Ali Dizaei is a Chief Superintendent in the Metropolitan Police. Born in Iran in 1962, he moved to the UK in 1972. He studied law and is currently legal advisor to the National Black Police Association. He has three children.

Tim Phillips is a freelance journalist living in London. Among his previous books is *Knockoff: the Deadly Trade in Counterfeit Goods.*

NOT ONE
OF US

The trial that changed
policing in Britain for ever

Ali Dizaei

with Tim Phillips

A complete catalogue record for this book can
be obtained from the British Library on request

The right of Ali Dizaei to be identified as the author of
this work has been asserted by him in accordance with
the Copyright, Designs and Patents Act 1988

First published in 2007 by Serpent's Tail,
an imprint of Profile Books Ltd
3A Exmouth House
Pine Street
London EC1R 0JH
website: www.serpentstail.com

Designed and typeset at Neuadd Bwll, Llanwrtyd Wells

Printed in Great Britain by Clays, Bungay, Suffolk
10 9 8 7 6 5 4 3 2 1

The paper this book is printed on is certified by the © 1996 Forest
Stewardship Council A.C. (FSC). It is ancient-forest friendly.
The printer holds FSC chain of custody SGS-COC-2061

FSC
Mixed Sources
Product group from well-managed
forests and other controlled sources
Cert no. SGS-COC-2061
www.fsc.org
© 1996 Forest Stewardship Council

Acknowledgements

There are many people in my life to whom I will always owe a debt of gratitude, and I hope I have begun to give them the credit they deserve in this book; but I would like to give special thanks to my family, especially my father and Natalie, who were always there to help me. My thanks also go to the National Black Police Association – whose members may empathise with my experience – for its commitment in helping to create this book. I would also like to thank Ravi Chand, who never doubted me for a moment and never wavered in his support for me.

A.D.

Part one

Out of the blue

1 **Kicked out**

'There are a number of issues we need to put to you, Mr Dizaei. Please sit down.'

18 January 2001 should have been a good Thursday. It started with a meeting with Deputy Assistant Commissioner Andrew Trotter, who had unofficially been my mentor since I had joined London's Metropolitan Police Service, the 'Met'. He'd given me praise, told me I was doing well in the two years since I had transferred from neighbouring Thames Valley, and in this meeting, I believed that I was to be told that I was going to attend the Senior Command Course the following April. It's a course that was created to prepare the best police officers for the highest ranks in the force. I had made no secret of the fact that I desperately wanted to be a chief constable one day; I thought my assessments and achievements merited promotion. I had been told by Sir Paul Condon – the commissioner of the Met, the boss of the force – to apply for the Senior Command Course. He seemed to think that I should get my chance.

Later that day I should have been lobbying my fellow members so that I could be elected the president of the National Black Police Association. The election was due to take place on Saturday at Bramshill Police College, forty miles outside the city. Having sounded out my colleagues, I was confident that I would win. I was still only thirty-eight years old. In the newspapers I had been called a 'high-flier' and a future chief constable.

The previous few months had been exciting. DAC Trotter had

been encouraging my work as a superintendent in day-to-day charge of operations in Notting Hill, Kensington and Chelsea, a job which gave me command over 600 officers. It's a prestigious location, a lot of responsibility: for example, there are more than ninety foreign embassies in the area. Harrods is part of the beat, as is the Notting Hill Carnival.

Away from my operational responsibility, as legal advisor to the NBPA, I had been at the centre of some controversial debates. I was becoming accustomed to being quoted in the newspapers, or interviewed on the radio or television, and I'll admit that I liked it. Four weeks previously, the *Guardian* newspaper ran an opinion piece that I had written about how policing has to change in a society that contains lots of different races, religions and customs. Not everyone approved of my views, and I received a regular trickle of hate mail two or three times a month telling me, in the words of one of the milder letters, to 'clear off back to your own country, good riddance'; but you don't join the police force if you need everyone to like you.

At that time, the National Black Police Association attracted headlines, because we were determined to stir up a debate that was overdue: was the Metropolitan Police 'institutionally racist'? At the end of November 2000, I had made headlines by giving a speech accusing the police of the 'ethnic cleansing' of black and Asian officers from senior ranks. In December, I had criticised the home secretary for reinstating a policeman who had been sacked for calling a teenager a 'black bastard'.

Whether the hate mailers believed it or not, I wasn't an arrogant publicity-seeker. I wanted to make the police force a better place to work for everyone, and a better crime-fighting organisation which was sensitive to the needs of the community – all of the community. I wasn't out to undermine the police force; I wanted to do what I could to make it better, because whether the hate mailers liked it or not, it had to change. I felt that the public needed to see more police officers who were committed to change. I knew I had a strong service record in fourteen years in the British police, and I itched with ambition to be able to put my ideas into practice and make a bigger contribution to policing. I was a loyal, hard-working employee and being a police officer was all that I wanted to be.

My meeting that morning was in an office I knew well, at Canon Row, the headquarters for Territorial Policing in London, opposite the Houses of Parliament. When I had transferred to the Met two years previously, I worked as a staff officer for the assistant commissioner whose office it was, as a new and junior colleague in a strange office. On the face of it, everything in my career was going well.

Well, almost everything.

For several months I had felt friction at work: several times I found my immediate supervisor hovering outside my office door while I was on the phone. While I was recommended for jobs offering more responsibility, I was discouraged from applying for them by the people I worked with. I had even asked for a sideways move, without success. Today's meeting had been delayed twice, without explanation. Something was not right.

Recently, a friend had told me we were being followed as we walked along the street. I told her she was imagining it. A colleague had warned me that someone was 'out to get me'. I worried, but I didn't believe that even if the people who disliked the way I did my job were out to 'get me', they could do so, because I had done nothing wrong. This is Britain, after all.

As I prepared for the meeting, one final detail stood out as odd. The previous evening, I had been in a coffee shop when DAC Trotter's staff officer called me. He asked if I was definitely going to be present the following morning. Having been pushing for the meeting for weeks, I was surprised. It's not the sort of appointment you risk oversleeping for, so I assured him that I would be there; I was staying at my father's house in North London that night, so I wouldn't have to drive in from my house in Henley-on-Thames.

When I arrived on the fourth floor for my 8 am appointment, the door to DAC Trotter's office was closed. Three other officers were inside, having an early meeting. I thought uneasily about the call the night before. Quietly, I asked his secretary who was in there.

'CIB3,' she whispered, and offered me tea.

My heart started to beat faster. The Complaints Investigation Branch, known as CIB, was set up so that the Met could police itself. It identifies bad cops, and investigates them. Its staff are called 'rubber heels', because corrupt cops don't hear them coming.

The guys inside the closed office were from CIB3. It is now known more descriptively as the Anti-Corruption Squad. Set up in January 1998, its 180 officers and its £15 million budget were dedicated to implementing the 'Corruption and Dishonesty Prevention Strategy' – investigating and gathering evidence against corrupt police officers, usually without their knowledge. At the time it was set up, the Metropolitan Police commissioner had stated, rightly or wrongly, that there were 'between 100 and 250' corrupt officers in the Met, so CIB3 had a big target to aim for, and pressure to perform. Unless it found corruption at that level, many observers would assume there had been a whitewash. CIB3 had apparently recruited some of the Met's most talented and dedicated detectives to work for it.

They aren't the people you want to see talking to your supervisory officer immediately before you have a meeting with him, but I thought that I had nothing to fear. I have always been an honest policeman, to the point of mild paranoia: the swearing and threats I received in the internal mail told me that I wasn't universally popular among other officers. Not wanting to give my critics any ammunition, for years I had been careful not to break any rules or bend any laws.

If I could have seen the street in which I lived in Henley-on-Thames, fifteen miles west of London, I would have been even more uneasy. At 6.30 am, ninety minutes before my meeting started, anonymous 'Metropolitan Police sources' had tipped off the crime reporters of all the major British newspapers and broadcasters that I was about to become a major story, and since 7.30 am they had been arriving outside my house with their cameras ready to capture a record of the day's drama. My wife Natalie, as oblivious to what was happening as me, was inside getting my three sons ready for school, after which she would start her nursing shift at the Royal Berkshire Hospital.

I'd certainly have panicked if I had known that a mile away from Canon Row, at New Scotland Yard – the head office of the Met – the Central Casualty Bureau was about to open. The CCB is staffed by volunteers from inside the force – up to 200 at any time – and opens to handle communications during major disasters. The staff takes calls, coordinates surveillance intelligence, provides a single source of information, and makes sure that everyone is informed. For almost fifty years, it had coped with bombs, crashes and other crises. Today, the CCB was going to coordinate my personal major disaster.

The door of the office opened. DAC Trotter came out.

'Put down your tea and come with me,' he said.

Inside his office, a large mahogany table. I sat at one end. At the other end sat DAC Trotter. To my right, Assistant Commissioner Michael Todd, who is now the chief constable of Greater Manchester. To my left, Detective Chief Superintendent Robert Quick – now the chief constable of Surrey – who I knew because he was also due to go on the Senior Command Course.

Also, to my left, a man I had never seen before. He introduced himself as Detective Superintendent Barry Norman, from CIB. 'There are a number of matters we need to put to you, Mr Dizaei,' he said. 'Please sit down.'

As the senior officer present, AC Todd explained that he was going to serve me with a number of Regulation 9 notices. These notices, known as 'Reg 9s', set out allegations that are made against you as a serving police officer. No one involved in operational policing escapes a Reg 9 during his or her career, because when any member of the public makes a complaint, it has to be recorded and followed up. As part of the procedure, you are issued with a Reg 9 telling you what the complaint is. A Reg 9 doesn't mean you are a crook. It doesn't even mean you are suspected of being a criminal. Its function is purely to inform you that you are suspected of a disciplinary offence.

My mind raced. I'd had a run-in with a detective inspector in CIB two months previously: my car had been damaged by a hit-and-run driver on the M4, and the investigating officer was being slow in releasing the details to me for my insurance. I had lost patience with the constable, who I knew from my time in the Thames Valley force, before I joined the Met, and we had exchanged strong words in several emails. Soon afterwards, the CIB inspector informed me that the officer had made a complaint about my behaviour, claiming I had been aggressive.

An argument over a damaged car wasn't the sort of case to interest CIB3, though. CIB3 investigates large-scale corruption and dishonesty. It investigates the sort of things that were on the Reg 9 notices that DAC Trotter read out to me.

I could hardly believe my ears when he told me I was suspected of using drugs, of visiting prostitutes, accepting bribes, assault, being involved in the sale of the Ethiopian Embassy, accepting a free calendar…

It was a long list, but the most shocking part was the way DAC Trotter introduced it: 'I need to discuss the issue of suspension,' he said.

I was being suspended: it was a bad dream, the set-up for a Hollywood blockbuster or a bad practical joke. They didn't look like they were about to start laughing and slap me on the back. I hardly drink, and don't smoke, so the idea of me being a drug abuser was ridiculous. I had never visited a prostitute in my life.

I had been so careful to be honest in my work, and now these accusations were painting me as a dirty cop, or worse, a crook. My hands were shaking as I looked at the notices in front of me, and I felt as if I was going to burst into tears. DAC Trotter was still reading, but I could hardly comprehend what he was saying: something about being a threat to national security, and about visiting the Iranian Embassy without permission.

The accusations were getting stranger: 'Hang on a minute. That's not right, is it?' I said, interrupting DAC Trotter, who was in full flow. Deceiving the Black Police Association so that they paid an airfare for me, conspiring with an associate to influence legal proceedings against a nightclub...

He had good reason to know that the complaint about visiting the Embassy was rubbish: DAC Trotter had personally given me permission to visit the building when I had asked him two weeks previously. 'I'm not going to conduct an interview now,' he said.

He would have been interviewing me for days if he had: in all, there were twenty allegations against me. I had allegedly tried to deceive the company that insures my car; I had apparently used my influence to get discount on a Cartier watch. I thought they had mixed me up with someone else who looked like me. He sounded like a nasty piece of work. I was numbed by the adrenalin racing through my bloodstream, but knowing that at least one of the charges was a straightforward administrative cock-up gave me confidence. 'I deny every allegation you have read to me,' I said. 'It seems I have a lot of enemies, and I am going to find them. This is a wasps' nest of spurious allegations made up by them...you had better make sure you get your facts right.'

It was a grand speech, but was no use at all. 'We have officers outside various houses and we are going to raid them,' DAC Trotter said, 'including your home.' He asked for my house keys. I refused. Still trying to make some impression, I told him he would have to break in. He wasn't getting the keys to my house as well.

I asked who else was going to have their houses raided. He wouldn't tell me. I was worried about my father, who was seventy-five and seriously ill, recovering from cancer. I was genuinely afraid that the shock of police coming through his front door to investigate his son could kill him.

AC Todd asked me for my warrant card. Perhaps the first thing I heard for thirty minutes that didn't surprise me was when he told me that I wasn't going to go on the Senior Command Course in April 2001. He took my mobile phone and my pager, and asked for the papers in my briefcase.

Until then I thought I was being arrested, but AC Todd told me I wasn't. I was furious, and angrily refused to give him the briefcase. He had no legal right to ask me for it unless he arrested me, as he should have known. He thought for a minute, and changed his approach.

'Perhaps you would hand over the papers voluntarily?'

No way. I knew I didn't have anything very interesting in my briefcase. Certainly not the briefcase that a drug-taking, prostitute-using, thieving, fraudulent threat to national security might have, but they had me cornered, and I wasn't about to be bullied into anything. At nine years old, I had learned a hard lesson about bullies when I went to boarding school. The lesson was not to be intimidated, to keep your head and to fight back. This wasn't a stupid playground scuffle, though; this was my career and my integrity that they were threatening to take away. They told me that I had been under surveillance for 'some time'. This made me more confused, because I had no idea that my own employers had been investigating me while giving me positive reports about my work. Also, I reasoned that if they had been watching me, they would know what rubbish these allegations were, and so there would be no need for this charade.

This charade was drawing to a close. In the middle ranks in the police force we are all members of the Superintendents' Association, and I was given the name of a Supt Russell, who would help me deal with my disciplinary hearings. He was to be my official 'friend' in the force. An inspector came in, and escorted me on the humiliating journey to the ground floor. I felt, as I told the *Evening Standard* newspaper when its reporter asked me, 'kicked out into the street like a dog'. At least my colleagues hadn't arrested me, which wasn't much comfort, but it was all the comfort there was.

I felt dazed, I felt angry and humiliated, and most of all I felt alone. That part, at least, was wrong. I was being followed by fourteen undercover police officers.

With no telephone and almost no money, I simply didn't know where to go. I walked along the Thames, away from the Houses of Parliament, in the direction of Trafalgar Square. It didn't matter which direction I walked in, I had nowhere I could go. After all, the police were probably breaking into my home.

My home! I had to call Natalie and tell her. At Charing Cross station, I found a payphone and spoke to her. She was calm and rational, as she always is. I told her to follow the police while they searched, as by this time I was frightened that they would plant evidence. There had been isolated incidents where corrupt police officers in the past had tried to make a charge stick against someone they thought was guilty by bringing evidence with them, and pretending that they found it at the scene. These 'first aid kits' as they were often called had successfully secured convictions in the past. Ironically, investigating the corrupt officers who planted evidence and bringing them to justice had been a major coup for CIB3 soon after it was established. Now I thought that my family might become innocent victims. It was a leap of imagination – and nothing like that actually happened – but at the time it seemed no more preposterous than what I had experienced in the last hour.

Natalie told me that three vans were outside from the TV news. I told her not to speak to any journalists.

We agreed that I would not go home. Instead, I used more of

my loose change to phone a close friend, Elham Hashemi, who I knew as 'Ellie'. I had known her since 1981. Her mother's brother is married to my cousin, and our families in Iran know each other well. Ellie lived and worked in Southampton, where she was a postdoctoral research fellow at Southampton University Medical School.

The police knew I called Ellie that morning, as they knew I had called Natalie. They have a list of all the calls I had made from public phone boxes, which I have seen. How did they do this? I can only imagine that they had intercepts prepared on every public telephone in the area or used telephoto lenses while I was on the phone. Considering that the area contained some of London's most famous locations – as well as Trafalgar Square and the Houses of Parliament, there's Number 10 Downing Street (where the prime minister lives) and the Foreign Office only a short walk away – they could have overheard some more interesting conversations than my garbled request for Ellie to come and get me. With hindsight, the investigators had probably assumed I would get in touch with my drug dealer, or perhaps a major criminal contact, and arrange a secret meeting. Instead, I went for coffee in a local bookshop and stared at my twenty Reg 9s on my own. As the news broke, no one could contact me. CIB3 had my phone, and like most people who store their numbers on their handset, I couldn't remember the number of anyone else. In my state of mind, I could barely have told you my own name.

I went back outside and called Supt Russell, who had been appointed as my superintendent 'friend', my first port of call in the force after I was suspended. He, at least, was sympathetic. 'Oh dear,' he said, as I read out the accusations. He promised to call the next day, and told me all about the forms I would have to complete, and how the disciplinary process worked. If it wasn't exactly encouraging, I did feel I had one friend in the force.

I found out later from official police records that Supt Russell, far from being a neutral 'friend', had been part of the undercover investigation. I trusted him, not knowing he had been involved in the investigation into the charges that I had just heard about. He knew all about the suspicions a long time before I called him, and so his surprised sympathy was an act for my benefit. 'Oh dear,' indeed.

More coffee. I had time on my hands as I waited for Ellie to arrive. When I called Natalie, she confirmed that police officers were ripping the house apart, and twice as many journalists wanting the first interview with the wife of the disgraced police officer were outside the door. She was sticking close to the police officers as they searched her bedroom drawers, which gave one of them a chance to joke with her about her underwear. I waited for Ellie's car to arrive, anonymous among thousands of other Londoners in Trafalgar Square, but still with my police tail. Finally I spotted her, jumped in the car, and headed for Dean Street in Soho, about half a mile away. I wanted to see a lawyer.

I wasn't looking for legal advice: I was looking for my friend Eddie Parladorio, who worked at Schillings. It's a well-known firm, but not a criminal firm: it specialises in civil cases, and attracts a lot of high-profile libel work, representing celebrity clients. I did my law degree with Eddie, and while he might not have been able to tell me with authority about the strength of a criminal case against me, he knew a lot about the effect of publicity.

'You're already headlines,' he told me when I arrived. I was a celebrity for the day, leading the lunchtime news bulletins: top cop suspended. Allegations of inappropriate contact with prostitutes, deception, assault. Boxes and a computer taken from his house. In the eyes of the public, many of whom were hearing my name and seeing my picture for the first time, I was already guilty of something serious, and I hadn't even been arrested.

Eddie kindly and freely gave his time, but this wasn't a coherent meeting. I just wanted to talk freely about what the bastards had done, and I knew the police investigators couldn't bug a solicitor's office. I didn't have much to say beyond my anger and frustration, because I didn't really understand what I was accused of. Ellie waited in the car. I'm ashamed to admit that, carried away with my anger, I almost forgot about her until late in the afternoon.

When we set off again for Southampton, it was around 5 pm and already dark. I drove, gripping the wheel and keeping to a speed of around thirty-five miles an hour. I knew I would be followed, and didn't want to break any speed limits. If there was any pleasure in skulking away from London like this, it was in knowing how boring it must have been for the police to follow us.

Two hours later, we reached the south coast. In Southampton, I dropped Ellie at her house, and tried to settle my nerves. There's a pub on the corner of her road. I don't drink – except for an occasional glass of champagne at celebrations – but I'd seen people having a large whisky so they could get a grip on themselves. That's what I did. I don't know if it helped, but Ellie wasn't pleased when I showed up at her door a few minutes later. She's a much stricter Muslim than I am, and never drinks, and told me exactly what she thought of my behaviour, which wasn't much.

With the luxury of a telephone, I could find out what had happened to the people I knew. I called my father. When I had left his flat that morning, his son was a successful police officer, and now his son was being branded a criminal on every TV station, in the evening newspapers, and on the radio. He asked me in Farsi: 'What have you done?'

'Nothing. It's all lies,' I told him.

He burst into tears, and we cried together on the phone. It was to be more than two years until I was cleared, but he supported me the whole time, and never asked me again. The police hadn't raided his house, but forensic teams had searched my car, my locker at the David Lloyd gym in Kensington where I trained almost every day, as well as the offices of friends: Tony

Alam, the owner of the Paparazzi Café in Fulham Road, had his computer taken away, as did Nasrin Isanjabi, a travel agent from whom the Black Police Association had purchased a ticket to the US in my name. My friend Aized Sheik also had his house searched – for no other reason, it seems, than he was my friend.

There was little to do except watch the news. The reporters seemed to know a lot about the case – including one allegation which I hadn't been told about in my meeting with CIB. Apparently I was suspected of fraudulently arranging visas for illegal immigrants as well.

I went to bed early. I slept badly. I felt as if I had the flu, and even though I was exhausted, I couldn't get to sleep. On the other hand, waking up wasn't an attractive idea, unless I could wake up from this nightmare.

The next morning, Ellie took the day off. I wanted to buy myself a mobile phone, and we went shopping in Southampton, feeling miserable and paranoid. In the shopping centre, everyone seemed to be reading newspapers, and I was in all of them. 'Race cop in tarts and sleaze probe' was the *Sun* headline, which said I had been suspended 'over claims he got visas for illegal immigrants'. It said I was 'also accused of lying about an attack on his car and visiting prostitutes...If the claims are proved it would end the career of the Iranian-born high-flier, regarded as a darling of the liberal elite.' The liberal what? An anonymous police source said: 'It is about the integrity of an officer.' There was a picture of me, and another of the police carrying boxes from my '£250,000' house in Henley. Translation: how could an honest policeman afford a house like that?

The *Daily Mail*, a newspaper that had rarely had a good word to say about my work before, had the story it wanted, and threw everything into discrediting me: alongside my picture, and the report of 'inappropriate contact with prostitutes', I was a 'twice-married father of three' who 'likes to be addressed as Dr Dizaei'. It added: 'Outside office hours he can usually be found in designer trousers, loose-fitting shirts, cowboy boots and designer sunglasses.'

Sunglasses aren't very useful in London in January, but they completed the character sketch of a flash Arab, an Iranian gangster, a Muslim terrorist, a man not to be trusted, not least because of another significant detail in the story. Readers learned that 'his father once headed the secret service' in Tehran. In the real world, my father once headed the traffic police, but I had left the real world behind the previous morning, and it seemed my family was going to be smeared with me.

The other tabloid papers ran the story ('Top cop barred in probe', 'Police high-flier in corruption probe') with less malice. Natalie had spoken to the journalists, furious about what was happening to us. 'It's terrible to be suspended and not know why,' she told the *Daily Express*. 'Maybe someone has made an allegation against him and they have thought, "This is it. We are going to go for it." Perhaps some people thought he was dangerous and didn't want him as high in the police force.'

While Natalie's fierce loyalty to me was a sharp contrast to what I had experienced from my colleagues, it had disadvantages. It made the story more exciting for the press. 'Met officer's wife complains of "racist plot",' said the *Independent*. 'I've been expecting something like this to happen,' she told them, 'because of the colour of his skin and because he has done so well.'

At that point, the only colour I wanted to be was invisible.

At 6 pm that evening, I was still in Southampton, unable to face my neighbours of fourteen years in Henley, or the reporters camped outside my house. Ellie answered the door to three police officers. I already knew Supt Norman of CIB3. He was with Detective Sergeant Fox, who I would also get to know well, and a female officer.

'I suppose you know why we are here,' Supt Norman said.

'I can guess,' Ellie said.

They wanted to talk to me. 'We don't want to embarrass you in front of the neighbours,' Supt Norman told Ellie, who didn't want to let them into her home.

'I have nothing to hide,' she said.

They mistakenly took that as an invitation, wiped their feet on the mat and walked in. Ellie apologised for the mess. She had just moved in, she said.

'Yes, I know,' Supt Norman said, to her surprise. Apparently it wasn't just me who had been watched for the last few months. He told Ellie that she would have to be interviewed under caution about my case, at a police station, at some point in the near future. To impart this non-urgent information, he was making a round trip of almost 200 miles, rather than picking up a telephone.

Or maybe it was for this: 'Have you read the *Evening Standard*?' he teased Ellie, before leaving. 'There's a very interesting article in it tonight.' The article featured my wife, defending me again. Was this to try and turn Ellie against me?

As they knew a great deal about me, they obviously knew that at that time I had an unconventional marriage. Shortly after the birth of our third child, Natalie and I realised that we had fallen out of love. We decided not to get divorced, but instead to live in the same house, and bring up our children together. I slept in a separate room. We have both had sexual relationships with other people, about which we were honest to each other. While Natalie has met some of my female friends – and got on well with most of them – neither of us would bring a partner into our home nor involve the kids. One day, we would sell our house, divorce amicably, and go our own way, which is what has now happened. It was, I mistakenly believed, our own business.

It was not perfect, and it led to me being branded a 'Casanova cop' by the tabloid press, but in ten years Natalie and I could count the arguments we have had on the fingers of one hand, which not many conventionally married couples could claim.

Supt Norman obviously believed that Ellie was a mistress; one that he could turn against me by showing how close Natalie and I were. If Ellie had not been so furious, she would have laughed at how ridiculous the scenario was. Having known me for years, she knew all about my domestic life. As a practising Muslim, who chooses to wear the hijab to cover her head, there was no possibility in Ellie's mind that our relationship could ever become sexual. I enjoyed her company, and we would go out to a restaurant or for coffee and talk about everything, although our custom dictates that as a single woman it would have been inappropriate for her even to arrive or leave a public place with me. Open expressions of affection, like holding hands in the street, would have been inconceivable. We could have explained this, and saved Supt Norman the need to make his dramatic visit, but he didn't ask.

In the weeks and months that followed, my life was to contain a series of odd dramas that made no sense, usually with Supt Norman as the leading man, and often with choreographed press coverage of my supposed shame. I learned that sometimes the innocent do have something to fear, and how you can be made to feel like a guilty man when you have nothing to feel guilty about. The investigators tried to bully me into submission. I nearly cracked. Some days I would just lie in bed, depressed, suspended from the job I loved, frightened to death that I would be sent to prison, shunned by former friends who thought I was guilty. It was to be almost twelve months before I knew what I was to be charged with – a year in hell, during which I found out who my real friends were, and during which I discovered how hard it is to undergo trial by public opinion when you don't even know what you are meant to have done.

2 **Presumed guilty**

The Hilton Hotel on London's Edgware Road probably entertains a lot of guests who sign in under false names, like every hotel in the country, because for some reason they don't want to attract attention. A few days after I was suspended, I watched as 'Mr and Mrs Brown' registered for a room.

Unlike most daytime residents, the view, the minibar or the room service weren't important, though a large bed would be handy, because everyone needed somewhere to sit. In real life, 'Mr and Mrs Brown' was the ironic name for ten members of the National Black Police Association. We had met in the hotel lobby, but overwhelmed with the feeling that we were being watched, we squeezed into our hotel room to talk about what had happened.

I had been expecting to be the president of the NBPA by that time, but now I was asking Ravi Chand, the man who was due to be my opponent in the election, for help. Any chance I had disappeared with my warrant card when I was suspended. Now I was just another suspended police officer seeking help from his staff association, just as many others had come to me in the past when they were in the same position.

I didn't have a warm relationship with Ravi, as we were quite different in our personalities: where I was often confrontational and outgoing, he was quiet and diplomatic. It didn't help that we were competing for the same job, which had magnified the differences between us while we both thought we had a chance of getting it.

Before he could offer help, I had to answer the usual question, which a hundred people had asked me already. 'Is anything these bastards are saying true?' he asked.

'This is all rubbish,' I told him.

'Then don't say any more,' he said, 'we'll support you.'

And they did: one of Ravi's first acts as president of the NBPA was to publicly back me. If he had been wrong, it could have undermined the credibility of the entire organisation, and made him look like a chump. If he had sat on the fence until the allegations went away, and had decided quietly to sideline me, you couldn't have blamed him. Instead, the NBPA worked hard, at considerable cost to several of its members, to help me to discover the truth about the accusations against me, and to clear my name. In the next twelve months, many members might have privately cursed me, as being associated with my case caused them problems they would never have imagined. Not one of them ever criticised me in public.

Hiring a hotel room and sneaking in to avoid surveillance sounds like a story from the Cold War. Under totalitarian governments or in police states ordinary citizens find that they have been investigated by the authorities – not because of what they had done, but because of who they knew. In Britain we take it for granted that we are treated differently, and most of the time most of us are. From the moment of my suspension, however, a lot of people I knew, or who knew people who knew me, or in one case had once been in the same room as me, found that they had been investigated too.

The investigation into me that triggered this was codenamed Helios. By the time I was suspended, it had already been running undercover for eighteen months, and was to run for more than two years, at a total cost to the Metropolitan Police of £4 million. When you add the cost of the legal support needed to prosecute me, the cost to the taxpayer of Helios has been about £7 million, though the officers in charge still dispute this figure.

If my estimate is correct, every household in the country donated 30 pence to investigate and prosecute me, twice the cost of the investigation into the Soham murders, perhaps the highest-profile investigation of the last ten years.

I had a codename: Mozart. There was a secret Helios headquarters, a sub-police station in Kent with the unlikely codename of Miami, where information was collected and filed. As my friends and associates were drawn in, their pictures would be pinned up, next to the information gathered from undercover surveillance, interviews and background checks. There was a chart of all my 'partners', going back several years, with my picture in the centre and arrows to illustrate when we had a 'relationship'. From the names on the chart, it seemed that Supt Norman had assumed that any female I knew was a lover. A reporter from an Iranian newspaper, who I had met twice to be interviewed for an article, was also on the chart. When I was provided with copies of the paperwork that came out of Helios – it was a legal requirement when I had a court case to prepare for – it filled a room; we had to hire a truck to move it.

While Helios was conducted in secret, life for me had been routine. In the days, weeks and eventually months after 18 January, that routine was replaced by a series of events that made no sense. At the time I felt as if I was being persecuted; as if someone was out to put me in prison whatever the cost. Looking back on it I feel the same.

During the first months of my suspension, some friends were already quietly backing away from me. It's not a good career move, either inside or outside the police force, to be associated with a suspected bent cop. Already, two friends had had their computers seized, which made running their legitimate businesses almost impossible. The computers were checked, and the hard disks searched for potentially incriminating phrases in my case before they were returned.

Some days I lay in bed with the curtains drawn, worrying that at any time I was going to be raided again. At other times, I spent entire days in the Law Library at Southampton University researching my case and writing briefing documents for anyone who would give me a hearing. Meanwhile the Helios team, not restricted by having to keep their investigation secret, were busy. On 18 January, they told me that they suspected me of serious crimes, and more importantly, they had told the nation first through the newspapers. It was vital that they should make the allegations stick. In January, they had decided not to arrest me, which must have meant that they didn't have enough evidence to make a criminal charge against me. Their first priority would be uncovering that evidence.

There is a line that has to be drawn in any investigation into a suspected criminal. I've had to draw it many times in my working life. Television cop shows like *CSI* or *NYPD Blue* give the impression that the cops, obsessively following every line of inquiry, will eventually stumble on the lead which conclusively solves the case and catches the bad guy. Reality is much messier: every case contains many lines of inquiry that have to be followed up, which may then create many more inquiries, and so on. Unless someone in authority is making decisions as to which inquiries need to be pursued, and which ones can be ignored, the investigation would quickly be buried under an impossible workload.

The need for some kind of management control is even more urgent when the investigation is so complex that it is not even clear if there is a crime. Without clear objectives, it can become a fishing expedition which undermines the integrity of the officers involved. Senior investigation officers (SIOs) are trained to remain focused and not be diverted by trivial details for this reason – for example, it would be foolish to charge a murder suspect for not paying road tax.

This seems obvious – but apparently it did not occur to the

Helios investigators that accusing me of stealing a second-hand jumper or accepting a free calendar might look rather odd next to allegations of being a threat to national security or a drug dealer…

The police service is also an unusual organisation, because the further down the hierarchy you are, the more discretion you have. In other words, those operating on the front line have far more flexibility in the way they apply the law than the senior managers in charge of them. In a business, for example, senior managers and directors provide direction and guidance to the people who work for them. How the directors choose to do that, provided it is legal, is a matter between them and their shareholders. In the police organisation, a senior officer has to make sure that the principles of good policing and written codes of practice are being followed. How they are applied is up to the detectives and constables on the streets – but for the police force to function, there has to be a match between what senior officers want, and what the front line does.

On the other hand, police work is not a science, and police officers are not robots. They have to use judgement. Sometimes, with hindsight, there are inquiries that could have been made but were not, and lines of inquiry that were exhausted but produced nothing. There are ways in which the decisions made by the person in charge can backfire: the most serious is that criminals get away with it, not because they have committed the perfect crime, but because the evidence to convict them wasn't discovered. That's a failure of omission – we didn't do enough.

It is also possible to do too much. In that case, thousands of pounds can be wasted, and manpower that could be better used elsewhere is diverted into a fruitless search for evidence. This has another negative effect: a runaway investigation draws in hundreds of innocent people, and affects their lives. It destroys their trust in society, and convinces them that we live in a police state that is out to get them. An out-of-control investigation is a fishing expedition at best, and at worst a witch-hunt: the accused person is definitely guilty of something, we just have to work hard enough to find it. The investigating officers might sincerely believe that their suspect is guilty – but someone, somewhere, has to take responsibility for the whole investigation, and say, 'Enough'. Not every suspect is Al Capone.

The jargon for this is 'proportionality'. Judge for yourself whether operation Helios was proportional, whether someone should have said 'Enough' at some point in 2001.

Every action taken in an investigation has to be logged: the log is the official record of the investigation. Helios had several very big logs. When I eventually saw some of the log entries for Helios during my suspension, I had to read them twice to believe them. Many of them were marked 'sensitive and highly confidential'. Obviously Supt Norman didn't want many people to see some of these entries.

'Check Supt Dizaei's weight training belt,' said one, 'it has someone else's name on it. Has he stolen it?'

'Check for missing items at police stations where he has worked,' said another, 'then see if found in house search, e.g., laptop missing in Kensington.' If they thought I was corrupt, it's perhaps not too much of a stretch to imagine I might conceivably steal a laptop, and if I had, it would be a significant theft. On the other hand, another entry: 'stamps went missing in 1980s, is there any record of it? Can Dizaei be linked to it?' At Reading police station, Supt Bennett was surprised when CIB3 called to find out if I had been a suspect in the theft of a rubber stamp more than ten years ago.

The search of my house had not been fruitless: it opened up another line of inquiry. 'Check if Thames Valley [police] want to take action since Supt Dizaei was in possession of a police name tag from his days in that force. Was he in lawful possession?'

Fortunately for me, Thames Valley told CIB3 that it did not want to prosecute me for the 'theft' of my old name tag.

My local dry cleaner was asked 'if Supt Dizaei had got a discount for cleaning his jeans' by abusing my status as a police officer, after it discovered that I had objected to being charged £15, and offered £5 – as anyone is legally entitled to do. The police should have been offering their sympathy to me for being chiselled by my dry cleaner, not investigating it as a disciplinary offence.

The content of any speech I had made was examined, to see if it was 'deceptive' and could merit another discipline charge. For example, in a speech to an American audience, I had said that they may be familiar with Chelsea – an area under my command – by referring to Chelsea football team. According to the policy log this was a misrepresentation: Chelsea football ground was 100 yards into Fulham's command area.

I had a business card from an acupuncturist in my office. He got a call too asking what his relationship with me was, and when we had met. If he could remember, he had a better memory than me.

Some inquiries look like pointless wastes of time. I did not eat in the station canteen, because the food was not halal there, so it would have been against my religion to eat it. This gave rise to two actions for the anti-corruption officers. 'Ascertain provision of halal meat at the Met canteen' was one (answer: there wasn't any. They took statements from canteen staff to ascertain this). 'Research restaurants Supt Dizaei ate at to see if they sell halal meat' was the other – again, statements were taken from surprised restaurant owners about their meat supply.

Officers fanned out through London, and interviewed every restaurant that they could find I had eaten in, to be told, yes, the meat here is halal. Quite what I would have been guilty of, had they discovered non-halal food was being served, I'm not sure. It certainly has no place in a criminal investigation.

I employed a Manchester firm called Rowe Cohen as my solicitors. This is not surprising, as Rowe Cohen traditionally represents any superintendent in the police force who is accused of anything. It's highly unlikely that a firm of solicitors that deals regularly with police officers as clients would be corrupt, but CIB3 was being thorough.

'Research Supt Dizaei's lawyers,' the log says, '(when qualified as a solicitor etc.), the hotel and room they "allege" to be stating the rate he pays etc.' Again, quite what I would be guilty of if the lawyers on my case were found to have lied about their qualifications or inflated their expenses without telling me, I can't say. It might save time for future investigations to record now that they had, not surprisingly, told the truth.

These actions were annoying and if the whole thing had not been so serious, laughable. Other lines of inquiry were more insidious. Four of my friends were put under surveillance. All the claims I made on my household insurance in the previous fourteen years were examined for evidence of fraud. 'Call credit agency to see how much his father owes' was another action. As my 75-year-old father was living modestly in Harrow, convalescing from his cancer operations, they were hardly trying to find evidence for how he funded a playboy lifestyle. If he had owed a lot of money or a little, what could they have concluded, other than that it is surprisingly easy to abuse their authority to invade an old man's privacy?

One night in 2000 I had dinner with Ali Ghavami, the Liberian ambassador at large, who is based in London. Ali is a friend of my father, and an Iranian. One of my Reg 9s alleged that I had abused my status and interfered in a business dispute between Ali and his builder. By the time he asked for my advice, they were suing each other, and Ali told me that the builder had threatened him and his son. I had asked a local constable to reassure Ali, and keep an eye on him – which seems to me to be good policing, rather than a disciplinary offence. However, the investigators made background checks on the nine other people who just happened to be in the restaurant that night, performed computer database checks on their cars, and later visited them and interviewed them about their 'relationship' with me.

Another CIB3 investigation concentrated on my parking tickets. Had I tried to get out of paying any of them? Had I used the police national computer (PNC) to make illegal checks on anyone? Had I persuaded anyone to do the checks for me? Every 'immigrant' – actually, almost all British citizens with foreign-sounding names – I knew, all eighty-two, had their immigration files checked to see if I was running an illegal immigration racket. I had already been accused in the newspapers of 'fixing' visas, when all I had done was help two friends fill in a form that I downloaded from the Home Office website. They didn't lie on the form, and no one did anything illegal. Supt Norman could have saved his investigators a lot of time if he had realised that many of these 'immigrants' had come to the UK and become British citizens before I was born.

Had I helped my family and friends fill in forms? Of course I had. Understanding any country's visa system is a skill that immigrants need. When any member of my family or a friend wants to visit, I have to tell the British Embassy that is considering their application why they are coming, where they will stay, how they will support themselves and when they will go home before the visit is approved. It's a pain, but it is a pain that is shared by millions of expatriates all over the world but perhaps not by the officers in CIB3. Being able to fill in the government's own forms properly isn't a crime, it's an essential part of being an expatriate in London – as it is anywhere else in the world.

Whether the Met meant it or not, in the months following my suspension, I suffered from a campaign of intimidation. Thanks to CIB3's exhaustive interrogation of everyone it thought was connected with me – whether or not I had ever met them – I was constantly having to explain what was happening to friends, acquaintances and, most of all, to my family. It wasn't helped by the fact that all this time I didn't really know what was going on. I had no idea what was being investigated, and sometimes I couldn't make any sense of the questions the police were asking them. They were as concerned as I was, and all I could say was, 'I don't know.'

Legally, because I was only suspended and not arrested, Supt Norman didn't have to tell me anything. There are no rules which say they have to disclose information, or even that they have to reveal all their lines of inquiry at once. This can't explain the process that Supt Norman used to serve me with more Reg 9s, which became a bizarre and stressful ritual.

Just over a week after I was suspended, I was told by CIB3 that it had more Reg 9s to serve. I didn't want to go through the humiliation of attending a police station to do it, I didn't want the investigators in my home again, and having had enough of media attention, I wanted the process to occur somewhere anonymous. Supt Norman decided that the best place would be the lobby of the Meridien Hotel in Slough. Each time Supt Norman called to tell me he had more Reg 9s to serve, I would have to go there and meet him and two other officers.

The Meridien seems to serve a good breakfast – at least, that's what it looked like, as I would walk into the lobby, feeling sick, to meet my accusers. Supt Norman favoured the *Daily Telegraph* in the mornings, and with his two sidekicks, he would generally order a cafetière of coffee and some croissants. Having usually been awake most of the night in fear that I would be arrested, I was in no mood for breakfast. I would take my latest Reg 9s, and walk out again. Why it needed three officers to hand me a form telling me I should not have accepted two invitations to the Muslim New Year celebrations without first putting it in the gratuity book is beyond me. Perhaps the hotel breakfast was too good to miss. I would always leave the hotel promptly to call the

NBPA and Ellie, leaving Supt Norman sipping his coffee and reading his newspaper.

I did this on 2 February 2001, and again on 23 February. And on 11 April, and 3 May. Each time I thought, this is it. Finally I will find out what this hell has been for, the real purpose of this investigation. At least I could get some satisfaction from knowing that I had finally touched the bottom, rather than the constant feeling of dread that sapped my energy. Each time, I was left wondering why they had summoned me to the hotel, to be served with minor disciplinary notices. For example, one Reg 9 accused me of wearing my uniform to give a speech in Los Angeles. Apparently I broke the rules – even though I was invited as a policeman, talking about the future of policing. The Home Office paid my fare, and the Met knew that I was going, and why. Should I be punished for being proud to wear my uniform?

Each time I was presented with a relatively minor charge, I went through three emotions. The first was elation – I felt like laughing at the absurdity of an investigation created to discipline me for wearing my uniform, and at my own doubts leading up to each meeting. It reminded me that I was innocent and that it was me who should be making a complaint, not them.

That passed into relief. If this was all they could find, surely they would give up soon.

In turn, that gave way to the same mix of fear and doubt that I was learning to live with. They were not giving up, so it was obviously not all they could find. They must, I reasoned, be working on evidence of a major crime, the Big One, that one day they would present me with. I didn't at that time know how many people were working on the investigation, or to what lengths they had gone in order to find the evidence that I had done something wrong, but I could easily see how much effort was being put into painting me as a rogue. This couldn't, I reasoned, be about eating halal food or getting a discount on dry cleaning. I would sit in my car on the way home, searching for the memory of what I could have done to provoke them into this, without success. I was chasing shadows.

The elation I felt at each of my Meridien breakfast meetings would disappear, and I would be left to wonder what the Big One was, what they thought they knew, and when I would be let in on the secret. Supt Norman was the image of confidence, relaxed on the hotel sofa with his newspaper. He knew, I thought.

If the CIB3's tactics were designed to crush me and my friends, they didn't work. But they came close.

I wasn't going to do nothing, to sit and wait for other people to decide what happened to me. I wasn't going to give up without a fight. I had lost my official status and my credibility in the eyes of a lot of people, but although it seemed like it at the time, you can't be found guilty on the evening news. During the weeks after my suspension, I set out to do everything I could to prove that the accusations were a fabrication, a witch-hunt and a miscarriage of justice. Half of this was to prove it to other people, who were used to seeing me as a confident, tough man who wasn't afraid to speak his mind, and would have expected me to come out fighting. The other half – which you don't talk about at the time – is to prove to yourself that they really are wrong, and that you can rebuild your confidence. When you lie awake at night full of doubt and fear, you can remind yourself that someone else should pay for this, and that one day they will.

I had three weapons. The first was my legal training. With two degrees in law and a PhD, I knew how to research what was happening, and how to write a brief for the people who wanted to help me. The second was, and always has been, the unwavering support of the NBPA. I needed Ravi Chand, whose integrity was unquestioned, to present the results of that research to anyone who would listen.

Last, my work for the NBPA had given me experience in dealing with people who could help. From what I had read so far, the *Sun* and the *Daily Mail* weren't going to print anything favourable about me, so I would go to the newspapers that would. I would lobby my local member of parliament. I would contact, or help Ravi get in contact with, anyone at all who could help me. Perhaps if the public could see what had happened, the investigators would see some sense.

I had learned that the CIB3 had a briefing team, and so conducting the arguments in public was a risky strategy. I reasoned that there was a crucial difference in this case: I could point to the facts, which then pointed to my innocence. Against those, the anonymous slurs of 'Metropolitan Police sources' didn't look as impressive.

By April 2001 I needed to let as many people as possible know that the image of the corrupt, drug-addicted spy cop they thought they knew, based on the anonymous briefings of the Met's press officers when I was suspended, was a fiction. I had contacts at several newspapers, which had published articles written by me only a few months previously, before I was suspended. Although I couldn't do an interview with the press directly while I was suspended, I could do the next best thing, and brief others to speak to the press with the facts on each charge.

The Met's press office is formidable, and Chris Webb, second-in-command of the department of public affairs, had been given the task of preparing the media strategy. We had to respond with the same level of organisation, so Ravi and I sat down one weekend at my house and wrote our own strategy, which was approved by the NBPA, and which we stuck to.

The *Guardian* printed the details of all the outstanding disciplinary offences against me on 2 April, the day I should have been starting the Senior Command Course, under the headline 'Met officer strikes back in "racist witch-hunt"'. Each supposed offence was listed, and evidence as to why I was not guilty. It was a strong piece: I accepted three charges – that I had received some free tickets to a local event (as many officers do – they are routinely sent to stations as a courtesy); that I had driven a car with diplomatic plates for two days (is that a disciplinary offence?); and that I had worn my uniform in Los Angeles. The *Guardian* had contacted Lorraine Johnson, the British Consul for investment, who was there. 'There was nothing unusual about his performance,' she said.

Ravi – keeping to our media strategy – weighed in with a quote: 'It is not the norm to investigate alleged trivial offences if you suspect a senior officer of serious criminal offences,' he said. 'The only reason is if you fear that bigger allegations are crumbling. It's a racist witch-hunt.'

At the same time, the NBPA held a press briefing to give the Met a public ultimatum. If the Big One existed (and we were beginning to think that after all this, it didn't), we wanted to know. Or, as Ravi challenged the Helios investigators: 'Put up or shut up.' The press conference, held only a few yards from New Scotland Yard, was well attended. Maybe it wasn't only the NBPA who thought that there was no Big One.

The next day, Met Police 'sources' were in the press again, alleging that I had been 'totally and utterly out of control', that my conduct had been 'absolutely horrendous', and that the investigation had been hampered because 'the Iranian community had closed ranks'. This pattern of briefing and counter-briefing was going to continue for two years. The more my friends said in public, and the more evidence my supporters provided to support my case, the more the CIB3 spinners whispered behind the scenes that I was guilty of *something*. Their tactics meant that they never had to limit the accusations to specific offences, or provide proof; and so I could never rebut their accusations.

It was a bitter, underhand war: my evidence was countered with their innuendo. I presented facts, they struck back with gossip and rumour. Perhaps we expect it of politicians or pop stars. When the country's largest and oldest police force conducts anonymous briefings against one of its own officers, something, in my opinion, has gone badly wrong.

The process of smearing my name reached a low when Lee Jasper, the mayor of London's policy advisor for equality and policing issues, was invited to a meeting with Supt Norman. Supt Norman had originally invited Ravi Chand to sit in on the meeting – but Ravi declined, as the NBPA had by this time made a formal complaint about his conduct, and so felt it was inappropriate. The two of them met, at Jasper's office. Jasper argued that the investigation was going nowhere, and that the facts the Met could present showed there was no case against me.

'This is nothing,' Supt Norman said, 'we've got something much bigger on Dizaei. And it will embarrass the NBPA.'

Maybe this was the Big One. Jasper asked what this bigger allegation was. After he heard the reply, he called Ravi and demanded to see him immediately.

When Ravi and his NBPA colleague Dave McFarland arrived at Jasper's office, there wasn't much talking. Jasper was concerned that his office might be bugged, and so he insisted on writing down the allegation in Ravi's notebook. What Ravi saw shocked him: if it was true, he had committed a serious error of judgement in backing my case.

Ravi and Dave McFarland walked around St James's Park, reading what Jasper had written in the notebook: '14 year old rape, assault, Dizaei and another.'

At that time, he assumed the Met was accusing me of raping and assaulting a fourteen-year-old. Or it could be that the police had uncovered a rape allegation from fourteen years ago. Whatever the interpretation, there was no positive way to see it.

'So this is it,' Ravi remembers saying to Dave, 'the rabbit out of the hat.'

They were shocked: Ravi had bet the credibility of the NBPA on a suspected rapist. All the other allegations didn't matter any more – no one would care. And no one was going to believe the word of a sex offender against the police. They walked on.

Then it occurred to them: if I was really suspected of rape and the police had evidence, why the blizzard of Reg 9s? Why pursue investigations into whether I ate halal meat? I would have been arrested at least, and charged with rape. They decided that Supt Norman wasn't doing my supporters a favour, making sure they didn't offer their support to a rapist. He was raising the stakes in the war of words. Afterwards I discovered that this bizarre allegation had been made opportunistically by someone who was questioned about me as part of Helios – but the officers involved had decided not to pursue it, as they would if the allegation had any merit. In that case Supt Norman should not have dragged out something as flimsy as this, and discussed it casually with Jasper. I can only assume that it was a desperate attempt to persuade him to back their case.

Ravi decided to ask me to come and see him at his office at Bedfordshire police headquarters in Kempston. He showed me the notebook. I was devastated. I made a copy of the page in the notebook, and still have it. But despite all the evidence that CIB3 prepared into my conduct, there is no further mention of this allegation, no further investigation into it, nor any conclusion drawn from the investigation. With hindsight, the allegation backfired on CIB3. It galvanised the NBPA's support, and made us all think: was there nothing that the Helios investigators would not accuse me of?

3 **The Big One**

CIB3 couldn't ignore the challenge to 'Put up or shut up' for ever, and at the beginning of May 2001, it looked as if it was going to shut up: there was no 'Big One' after all. My solicitor Ian Lewis called with good news. He had spoken to Supt Norman, who had told him that I wouldn't be charged with anything criminal. Instead, I would be disciplined internally.

I was excited. After five months of investigations, CIB3 had not even found anything to arrest or charge me for. It was clearly a disaster for CIB3. It had quietly dropped the allegations that I was sleeping with prostitutes (which, it transpired, had been made after surveillance overheard a friend teasing me that 'the only girlfriends you get are the ones you have to pay for'), and many of the other Reg 9s that had made such juicy headlines – although I was still threatened with discipline for receiving a free calendar, among other transgressions. Now I wanted revenge, to take my accusers to an employment tribunal. My life had been ruined. Someone would have to be held accountable, and then I could get back to being a police officer.

Two days later, Lewis called again. Supt Norman had called him.

'I would be failing in my duty if I didn't put some questions with regard to criminal matters to Supt Dizaei under arrest,' he had said. Perhaps someone had realised the public relations consequences of making this a matter of internal discipline. BBC News had given

them a hint by allocating fifteen minutes to the case, detailing
how the allegations were being dropped, one by one.

Being arrested didn't mean I would necessarily be charged
with a crime – but it was serious. In British law, the police
have to 'reasonably suspect' that an arrestable offence has been
committed, and in 2001 that meant either that the maximum
prison sentence for the offence would be five years or more, or
that the offence fell into one of several categories of serious crime,
such as public order or theft. There is a right to silence if you're
arrested. I wouldn't have to say anything – but, as I had warned
hundreds of people I had arrested in the previous fifteen years, 'it
may harm your case if you fail to mention something which you
later rely on for your defence in court'.

My elation switched abruptly to despair. I thought I was soon
going to be vindicated, and two days later someone, somewhere in
the Helios hierarchy changed their mind. Whether this was done
to save face, or whether it was done because someone genuinely
thought I had a case to answer, I'll never know – although if there
genuinely was a case to answer, why was I almost let off the hook
forty-eight hours earlier?

Ultimately, it didn't matter who was in charge of the decision,
I was still going to be arrested. Lewis offered that I would come to
the station for a 'voluntary interview': it's a common procedure,
avoids an unnecessary arrest, the interview would be recorded,
and it happens all the time.

No, I was to be arrested.

So this was it: the Big One. I was nervous, but at least I would
soon know what my personal hell was all about. The questions
I was asked in my interview would show what the Helios team
thought it had.

At 9 am on the morning of 11 May 2001, I arrived at Charing
Cross police station with John Swarbrick, a solicitor from Rowe
Cohen, who was representing me. Supt Norman met us in the

lobby with three other officers, pleased with himself. He could question me for sixteen of the next twenty-four hours in his custody suite, during which time I couldn't contact anyone.

'I am arresting you for deception,' he said, 'in the purchase of tickets to Los Angeles. The circumstances are that you bought the tickets for £340 and charged the NBPA £688.'

This was for travel to the same conference where I had earned a Reg 9 for wearing my uniform in public. Again, I was excited.

To make this an arrestable offence, it had to be categorised as 'obtaining property by deception' with a huge potential financial gain. Most senior police officers wouldn't consider an arrest when the financial gain was £344. I wouldn't have, but this investigation, not for the first time, was different.

I had obtained the property, but I couldn't see where the deception was. I had bought the ticket from my friend Nasrin Sanjabi. She had paid £340 for the ticket, and made a profit from selling it to the NBPA. I had paid £688 for the ticket, because that's what she did for a living. Nasrin was a travel agent, running a company called Arya Travel. As most people would immediately recognise, this is how travel agents make money, whether or not you know them.

It seems she wasn't even making as much money as most travel agents. Because the NBPA was paying for the ticket, I had called around to find who was cheapest, and it had been Arya. Nasrin also let the NBPA pay on invoice – sometimes several weeks later – rather than in advance, understanding that the NBPA was funded by the Home Office. By any standards, the NBPA was getting a good deal.

This simple explanation wasn't going to be enough for CIB3. As I sat in the interview room at Charing Cross – a tape recorder, a desk, chairs for Swarbrick and me on one side, chairs for the police on the side where I usually sat – Nasrin was walking to work in Kensington, central London. Three police cars pulled up at high speed, stopping her. Officers jumped out of the cars to arrest her, and took her to a different interview room in a different police station.

The police logs show that CIB3 investigated the possibility of 'cross-wiring' the interviews – in effect, putting a central command office in touch with both interview rooms, so I could be questioned on what Nasrin revealed, and she could be asked about what I said. It's a valuable technique for breaking down murderers, armed robbers and terrorists, but in this case it wasn't technically possible. And perhaps someone thought that for a possible deception of £344, it might be overreacting.

When arrested and questioned, there's a great temptation to explain yourself, especially when the officers might selectively quote from the transcripts of telephone conversations that they have recorded. I could have told Supt Norman that the cheque from the NBPA was to Nasrin's company, and that no money went from her company, or her account, to me. I could have explained that she was my friend. I could have told them to look at their own investigations into the finances of my father and the rest of my family to try and find the mysterious £344 backhander that I had received, because it wasn't there.

Swarbrick was as surprised as me to hear what I had been accused of. With what they had, they should have been arresting everyone who buys anything from a shop where they know the shopkeeper. 'No offence has taken place,' he said, 'don't say anything.'

I drew a cross on the whiteboard on the wall in my line of sight. I stared at it. I knew if I spoke I would be tempted to shout and scream, so I said nothing at all, except once, when Detective Sergeant Fox, who was leading the interview, became aggressive and belligerent.

John had to remind him that I was still a supervisory officer. I had been arrested, but I hadn't been charged. I was suspended, but I was still in the police force. There were rules of courtesy he should have been following. In truth, I was reminding myself to keep calm as well.

DS Fox's monologue dragged on. If it had been happening to someone else in an interview room at a station I was running, I'd have been appalled. To me he seemed overwhelmed by the volume of information at his disposal. It felt as if an inexperienced schoolteacher was trying to question a student. The interviewing officer should disclose all the relevant information before starting an interview. It's the right of someone accused of a crime to see what he or she is accused of. After a few hours of no response from me, away they went, and came back with a few more files that they could have shown to us at the beginning of the interview. Swarbrick and I read them. They contained transcripts of telephone taps, translated from Farsi, which they obviously thought demonstrated some sort of criminality.

'Do you think you should be cooperating with us now?' Supt Norman asked, after we had read pages of pointless phone transcripts which contained nothing incriminating that I could see. It was like a practical joke.

When friends complained about what they saw as their persecution by the British establishment, I usually had an answer: 'Things like that don't happen here.' I was, or I had been, a part of that establishment. We have rules about how people accused of crimes are questioned: rules like giving that person all the relevant information at the start of the interview. Another one is that after six hours in custody, the duty inspector has to review the detention, to see if there is any point in proceeding.

So, six hours into the interview, the duty inspector walks in. 'I am authorising your further detention,' he says. I could not resist pointing out to him that the police code of practice, which at that point governed my rights, states that the detained person and his lawyer 'should be given an opportunity to make representations before detention is authorised'. He conceded the point, and left the room, followed by my interviewers, for twenty minutes. When he returned, Swarbrick told them clearly that in his opinion my detention was a sham.

The duty inspector leaves, then pops in again a few minutes later. He's authorising my detention.

Still, there's no point in saying anything. The allegation makes no sense. After nine hours, a few more documents appear that add nothing to their case. After fourteen hours, we got a break from the arduous business of staring at the wall, which made a change. Then we went back to the one-sided interrogation for the final two hours.

With minutes before he had to release me or charge me, Supt Norman let me know that I was free to go.

'You'll get a decision from the Crown Prosecution Service in three days,' he said.

In Britain, when the police charge you with a criminal offence, the Crown Prosecution Service manages the prosecution process. The staff of the CPS decide which cases are worth prosecuting and what the charges should be, which barrister should be doing the job, and when the court case will take place. The CPS works alongside the police – and of course listens to the arguments that investigating officers put forward, but it does not work *for* the police: just because a police force wants to prosecute someone, the CPS doesn't automatically do it. It has to take a view on whether there is a realistic prospect of a conviction, and whether it is in the public interest to prosecute. It can tell the investigators that they need more evidence, or it can simply say: 'No'. Having been on the other side of the table, I knew that the 'three days' Norman promised was a smokescreen. The CPS had already said 'No', because there was no new evidence to consider after my interview. It wasn't interested in prosecuting Nasrin and me for selling and buying a plane ticket, not surprisingly.

It was now 1 am on 12 May. On 11 May 2001, the police minister of the time, Charles Clarke, told parliament that just 25 per cent of the offences recorded in England and Wales in 2000 had been solved – meaning that a likely offender had been identified and an arrest made in one of four cases reported to the police. More than 3.9 million crimes from the previous year were unsolved. The crime clear-up rate had fallen by 4 per cent in the previous year, and by 7 per cent since 1990. Also on 11 May 2001, the British transport police sent a questionnaire to 2,100 officers asking if they felt they disliked people with ginger hair, limp handshakes or hairy backs.

And also on 11 May 2001, I sat in silence for sixteen hours, while two of the Met's senior detectives, supposedly the cream of the force, interrogated me for the crime of buying a £688 plane ticket.

I left custody tired, but elated. My parting gift was in my hand: a letter that told me that no further action was to be taken on many of the charges that the CIB3 had used to smear me in the press. The embarrassing accusation that I had used prostitutes, the strange fiction that I had interfered in Ali Ghavami's civil dispute, the allegation that I used my position as a police officer to get a discount on a £2,000 Cartier watch, and the disciplinary charge that I visited the Iranian, Liberian and Ethiopian embassies without permission were all history. I had never even been questioned about them by the police, although some of the officers involved had been happy enough to discuss them with reporters. In 2005, the Morris Inquiry,* an independent inquiry into professional standards in the Metropolitan Police Service, found that reporters had been briefed in advance by police officers, and recommended that this practice should cease.

* http://www.morrisinquiry.gov.uk. The report sections 10.63 to 10.66 deal with this practice, and 10.76 clarifies the recommendation.

Needless to say, CIB3 didn't issue a press release this time, as it had when it made the accusations.

Outside the station, a group of colleagues who had come to support me were waiting. We went to a nearby hotel to celebrate, briefly, as I was too tired to talk to them sensibly about what had happened. I told them I would give them the details the next day.

The Met's Department of Public Affairs (DPA) had one further surprise for me. While I was in custody, the *Sun* was finishing another story about me. 'Top policeman arrested for £20,000 fraud,' it said. None of my accusers were quoted by name.

After that, I'd had it with my employers, CIB3, Operation Helios, the spin doctors of the DPA, Supt Norman and his helpers, the small army of timewasters and yes-men who had conspired to interrogate Nasrin and me. I was, and am, a loyal police officer. Staying quiet in the face of this provocation was too much to ask me.

With the NBPA, we held a press conference on the Monday. Ravi was tough. 'The sleaze allegations were leaked to discredit Mr Dizaei in the community,' he told reporters, 'whilst the visits to foreign embassies were used to put doubts in the public's minds about issues of national security to justify the overreaction to this case. We condemn this racist spin which puts a serious doubt on the integrity of this investigation.' He called on Deputy Commissioner Ian Blair, then London's second most senior policeman – he's now the commissioner, and so is still my boss – to resign. The NBPA had agreed this would be our strategy – but only if we saw no alternative.

With hindsight, that press conference was the time when things got nasty. It was the time when I gave up hope of an amicable solution to the whole thing: part of me had hoped for a very British conclusion, where we could have agreed that things went a bit far, and shouldn't happen again, and the people who had done this could apologise and accept the blame, and I would go back to work, and we could move on. Perhaps if the NBPA hadn't called for the resignation of the number two policeman in London, that could have happened.

Perhaps arrogantly I believed then that the coverage would force the CIB3 to 'shut up' – to drop Helios altogether, because they surely could not charge me with a criminal offence. Again, I was in for an unpleasant surprise – but not nearly as big a surprise as my colleague Chief Inspector Leroy Logan, the chair of the Metropolitan Black Police Association.

In 2001, Leroy was, as he still is, a dedicated policeman. He had been awarded an MBE by the Queen for services to the community and was a likeable, honest and sincere man, as almost everyone agreed. Almost everyone, that is, except CIB3.

With hindsight, you don't call for the resignation of the deputy commissioner of the Metropolitan Police and expect nothing to happen. If we were naive, we didn't expect the Met's next move. CIB3 called Ravi in May 2001 and asked to check the NBPA's accounts for any transactions with the Arya Travel Agency, as part of the investigation into me. Ravi refused: any request would have to go through the NBPA's lawyers.

The NBPA's offices were at that time on Queen Anne's Gate, as is the Home Office building, less than 100 metres from New Scotland Yard – from where Supt Norman called and wrote to Ravi Chand to ask for the documents. When Ravi objected to producing them, Supt Norman simply ignored him. Supt Norman ordered his officers to go to the accounts department of the Home Office to load a van with NBPA files and then to check every transaction that the NBPA had done with Nasrin. There was no warrant or court order.

The NBPA immediately complained to the permanent secretary of state for the Home Office for allowing this to happen. The NBPA warned the Home Office of the potential damage it could cause to their relationship.

Arya Travel had also sold the NBPA tickets to go on an official trip to Chicago. Again, Helios officers checked the mark-up. They checked whether Nasrin was more or less expensive than other travel agents. We could have helped: the Home Office funded the trip. It was personally authorised by Jack Straw, at that time the home secretary. The Home Office helpfully suggested a guide price for the tickets, and we had prepared a list of quotes. Arya Travel gave us the cheapest price.

Instead CIB3 now hired a firm of accountants to look at every financial claim that I had made from the NBPA since 1998. Every taxi driver who had given me a receipt was traced and statements taken. Every petrol receipt I had submitted was audited.

You can perhaps make a case for doing this in the barmy world where investigating a mark-up on my plane ticket is worth arresting someone for. If there's a pattern of deception, perhaps you might find some clues in my taxi receipts. And if I had submitted fraudulent expense claims, I was stealing from the Home Office – and ultimately from everyone who pays taxes. The irony was that the funds I had allegedly stolen also belonged to the NBPA. The NBPA would have presumably been the victim of any crime, but it had not complained. Indeed the NBPA wasn't a bit grateful when Supt Norman embarked on his search for justice on the organisation's behalf.

Even in that mad world, what the Helios investigators did next has no justification. Instead of limiting the search to my expenses, they decided to give the accountants a bigger job: auditing every expense claim made by key members of the NBPA executive during the period. Without consulting the NBPA, it asked for permission from the Home Office to go through the books of the NBPA, and investigate everyone they found. And this is how they netted former NBPA chair, Chief Inspector Leroy Logan.

In 2001 Leroy, who had defied his father and friends to join the police at the age of twenty-six, had served for eighteen years in the Met. His father had been disappointed when Leroy joined the force, because he had been beaten up once by police officers. He thought that Leroy was turning his back on his own community. We had worked closely together as chair and vice chair of the NBPA when it was set up, trying to help the Met and the police service to stop good black police officers from growing disillusioned and leaving. I had preferred the limelight, but we had worked well with the same goal. His considered tone was extremely effective in the press. There was no one who suspected Leroy of being dishonest – outside CIB3. Perhaps they reasoned that an officer like him, who worked alongside an officer like me and had supported me throughout, must be guilty of something.

On 10 November 1999, Leroy had stayed at a hotel in Manchester on BPA business. Sometimes we paid our hotel bills ourselves; sometimes they were paid for us by the association. If Leroy was guilty of anything, it was not doing his expense claims often enough; and three months later, he accidentally claimed for the hotel bill when he submitted his expense claim. It was the last week of his tenure as chair of the Metropolitan BPA, and so all his outstanding receipts had to be filed. We've all done it. He claimed for his hotel bill, but it had already been paid by his association, though at the time it hadn't been made clear to Leroy that would happen.

The total bill was £80.

On 29 June 2001 Leroy was on a course in Arundel, West Sussex, attending a lecture. Supt Norman personally drove 100 miles and called him out of a lecture he was attending to hand him a Reg 9 notice about the expense claim. He wanted to serve Leroy with the notice in the foyer. Leroy asked if Supt Norman could serve the notice in his car.

'Why are you taking such a formal approach?' he asked Supt Norman. It was unprecedented in Leroy's experience, and embarrassing.

'We have to treat you the same as Ali Dizaei,' Supt Norman said.

Leroy was mortified to be accused of fiddling his expenses. He immediately apologised, looked into what had happened, explained and paid back the £80. It was his fault, he admitted, but he hadn't done it on purpose. Instead, he was detained and interviewed on 24 July 2001 for three hours over his hotel bill. Leroy took a different approach to mine. He cooperated fully, answered every question, and never invoked his right to silence.

Not surprisingly, there was no charge to face. Later the charges were quietly dropped, but not until 14 November 2001, almost six months after he was served with his Reg 9. Another two years was to pass, and the threat from Leroy to go to an employment tribunal, before his complaint over the way he was treated by his own employers was finally settled. The Met offered him £100,000 and an apology. He took it, on condition that they also looked into other cases where he thought officers had been singled out unfairly. His parents were both more than seventy years old when he was arrested, and he had to explain to them that he had not abandoned his principles and started stealing from his employers. They both died before the tribunal was settled.

Later, Leroy told a public inquiry: 'Building reputations can take a long time, but you can lose them in a second...that was a great hurt not only for myself but also for my wife and children. It is really difficult to explain to your son that daddy is not going to prison... I would never jeopardise the reputation of myself, my family and the organisation for such a matter. It was clearly an oversight.'

Others close to me suffered from the need to bring a charge, any charge, against me. One of the worst-affected victims was Ellie, who is an unlikely criminal: she is honest, hard-working and cautious. Ellie and I don't talk now; the pressure of Helios and the negative publicity she received in a press which characterised her as part dupe, part mistress and part concubine destroyed the close supportive friendship that we once had – a friendship that the nudge-nudge newspapers could only write about in the most sordid terms at the time.

The Helios officers too regularly called Ellie at home and at work. The calls started on the Sunday after I was suspended, at 9 am when Ellie was visiting her family in London. DS Fox was reluctant to identify himself to her, but she insisted. He asked to speak to Ellie's mother: they were following a lead which eventually led nowhere, but Ellie's mother, who had been partially paralysed by an accident, and who had very little English, was getting dragged into the investigation too. DS Fox and two other officers – one a female Farsi-speaking interpreter, the other a Helios officer named Buttivant, turned up on the doorstep two hours later, and took Ellie to one room, and her mother to another.

Buttivant questioned Ellie on our relationship, 'so that we don't say something we shouldn't in front of your family.' If this was a ham-fisted way of avoiding embarrassment for Ellie, it was particularly incompetent: to have the three officers in the family house was quite humiliation enough for a Muslim woman. 'If you are suggesting I am having a sexual relationship with Ali Dizaei, I am not,' she told Buttivant after he asked if her 'family was aware' of Ellie's 'relationship with' me. Ellie tried to rejoin her mother. DS Fox said that he didn't want Ellie in the room while he spoke to her mother, much to the shock of Ellie's mother, and he later told Ellie, in front of her family, that he would be contacting her the next week in relation to some criminal charges. Ellie's crime, as far as she knew, was simply to be my friend.

Ellie was outraged. She contacted a firm of solicitors, who told her not to go to a police station unless one of the officers responsible told her why she was going there. If not, the solicitor advised, she should refuse to go unless they arrested her. Meanwhile, DS Fox took to occasionally phoning Ellie for a chat at work, always identifying himself to her nonplussed secretary. When Ellie used one of these calls to relay the advice from her solicitor, DS Fox told her why they wanted to speak to her at the police station: it was another investigation of obtaining pecuniary advantage by deception, based around an incident when Ellie borrowed my car for a week. Ellie could have been arrested for this 'offence' – so, reluctantly, she agreed to go to Southampton police station, scared and confused, to answer questions. Her solicitor even had to warn her it was best not to leave the Southampton area. If she went to visit her family in London, he explained, she could be arrested on the Met's turf, and he wouldn't be there to help her.

The offence sounded serious: and it could have been, if there had been a case to answer. Ellie didn't find this out until 13 February 2001, when at 5.30 pm she walked into Southampton police station for her interview. Her solicitor, as is his right, asked for full disclosure of all the facts around this charge before the interview. Ellie waited in the interview room for fifty minutes on her own, trying to find in her memory a hint as to what she was supposed to have done.

Her solicitor returned to see her. 'They have nothing to show you have committed an offence. They just want to get you in there and ask you questions to incriminate Ali Dizaei,' he said. 'If you want my advice, stay away from it and just walk out.' Which she managed to do.

The reason Ellie was being stalked like this: almost two years previously, in a taped telephone conversation that she has no recollection of to this day, she said, 'Yeah'.

In August 1999, Ellie had damaged her car, but needed to use a car to visit her sick mother in London. She was marking PhD papers, and so she didn't need a car for work, because she was at home during the day. I agreed to lend her my BMW.

She had fully comprehensive insurance, so she was entitled to drive my car, but she asked me to add her as a temporary driver on my insurance as well as an extra precaution. When I called the insurance company, they reminded me that Ellie couldn't use the car for work. I called Ellie, and speaking in Farsi, reminded her of this.

She said, 'Yeah'.

At least, in one version of the conversation, she did. There are three transcripts of this conversation. In one, she says, 'Yeah'. In another, we pass on to another conversation. In a third incriminating version, it might possibly sound as if I'm hinting to her that even if she was using the car for work, she should pretend that she wasn't, and she agrees.

Three versions, three translators. I later discovered that after criticism of the first translation, which looked pretty accurate to me (a word-for-word translation from Farsi to English is impossible, as the two languages have a completely different structure, so every translation will have an element of interpretation in it) the Met asked for two more translations to be done by Farsi-speaking officers. These officers were working on Helios, and should not have been employed as translators, as there is a clear conflict of interest. The accuracy of one of the translations was later challenged in court.

Ellie's 'yeah' may or may not have been consciously said. If it was conscious, it was simply her acknowledgement that my insurance didn't cover the car for driving to her office, where she wasn't going anyway. This had become the basis for a criminal investigation. Were we defrauding the insurance company? As she hadn't crashed the car – or made any claims – and as the car was insured already through her own insurance cover, it's not exactly the work of two criminal masterminds in cahoots. Even a first-year law student could see there was no crime here. If it wasn't so serious, it would have been laughable.

Ellie's solicitor wisely told the Met not to contact her; CIB3 kept calling. Ellie wasn't sleeping, was frightened that she might be arrested at any time, and fearful of what would be in the newspapers about her, having become one of my 'mistresses', much to the shock and dismay of her traditional family. Eventually, she tired of the constant fishing expeditions, the humiliation and embarrassment, and launched a formal complaint against the investigating officers which is still ongoing. Needless to say, she was never arrested or charged.

One clue about where the investigation was heading came from Ellie's slow torture. On 14 May 2001, two days after Nasrin and I had been interrogated, Ellie was about to leave for work. At 8.45 am, Buttivant called her. As an experienced detective, he said, he was investigating an incident where my car had been scratched. His experience told him it wasn't an accident, he said, and perhaps was done by a former girlfriend. Did Ellie know that I had been 'arrested with my girlfriend'? Did Ellie have anything she wanted to tell him about who might have done it? He had to do his job properly, he said, and so had to investigate this criminal damage.

Ellie remembered the scratch well, because I had called her at work when it was done, blowing off steam as she listened patiently to me ranting.

As she listened to the detective casually telling her that in his personal view, she was probably guilty of a criminal offence, Ellie's patience snapped. 'Frankly,' she said, 'you're insulting my intelligence.' She wasn't going to be intimidated, she told him. Soon after, she sent the message that she didn't want to cooperate any more with the 'investigation'. The next she heard about this obscure scratched car was when I heard about it.

The scratched car, you see, was the Big One.

On the morning of 19 December 2001, eleven months into my suspension, I was told to attend Charing Cross police station once again for a decision on whether I would be prosecuted for paying Nasrin £688 for a plane ticket. On the tube from my dad's place in Harrow, I was working out that Nasrin, who had been told to go to the station earlier, would already know her fate. On 7 October, the *Sunday Times* had carried an article saying that the Met was going to bring criminal charges against me – my file had been passed to the Crown Prosecution Service for action. 'The revelation that his case has gone to the CPS will outrage those who claim he is the victim of a racist witch-hunt,' the article said.

Supt Norman was about to find out how outraged they were. Into the too-small lobby of the police station squeezed my lawyer John Swarbrick, myself, twenty members of the NBPA, TV cameras and press photographers. I was nervous, but the crowd that came with me was a mix of the resentful and the inquisitive. The NBPA representatives might have been police officers, but at that moment they probably looked like a crowd of angry black men spoiling for a fight. The investigation was taking on some nasty racial overtones, and to me Supt Norman was the personification of the enemy. When he came out to see us, the door slammed behind him.

Office doors in police stations, for security reasons, open only from the inside.

It was Supt Norman's turn to feel uncomfortable as he knocked and rattled the handle, trying to get into his own offices, while twenty black coppers laughed at him, and cameras recorded his embarrassment.

The next time, he bobbed only his head out, summoning Swarbrick and me to an interview room, where it was his turn to use backup. Five other officers hung around to see the rewards of their investigation. This, it seemed, had become personal for both of us.

Supt Norman awkwardly acknowledged that I wasn't going to be prosecuted for buying airline tickets. There was no charge of corruption. Nasrin would have just heard the same news, and would no doubt have been relieved. Her nerves were in shreds. The investigation had wrecked her health and seriously undermined her business in the last six months.

'But you are still going to court, Mr Dizaei,' he announced proudly, 'for the car and for your mileage!'

The criminal charges that they had me for were making false expense claims, perverting the course of justice and misconduct in public office.

The first set of charges was the purest fantasy, based on the trawl of the NBPA books: it wasn't that I had over-claimed, or handed in false receipts. It was that I had not always taken the shortest route to meetings.

The other summons, containing the other two charges, was the real Big One. I was to be prosecuted for lying about the location of my car when it was scratched. It didn't help that I had lied to the investigating officers on that day, and they knew it, because I had been under covert surveillance at the time. Perverting the course of justice is a serious charge with a maximum life sentence: police officers who have been convicted of it in the recent past routinely received sentences of two, four or even six years in prison. Very few convictions do not involve a custodial sentence. Misconduct in public office also carries a prison sentence, which can be as long as the crime is serious. There's no limit.

I had lied about the location of my car, but I had my reasons to fib. Good ones, as it turned out, yet it would be more than a year until I could defend myself in court, twenty-one months until there was a verdict, and three years until I returned to work. I might have done little wrong in my own eyes, and in the eyes of my supporters who were crowding rowdily into Charing Cross police station, but in the eyes of a powerful group of enemies, I was certainly guilty of something.

My life to that point had given me a thick skin: as an immigrant, a member of a minority community and a police officer I was no stranger to criticism and hostility. But this was different. Whatever I had done wrong in their eyes was serious enough that they wanted me not just humiliated and out of my job, but locked up as well.

I had an exemplary record in the police force. I didn't take bribes or cut corners. I had big ideas about how to improve policing, and one year previously I had been on the verge of putting them into practice as one of the most senior policemen in London. I had come to the Met Police as the commissioner's golden boy, on his personal request, an ambitious officer with a bright future.

It's not my habit to sit and brood, but at times there wasn't much else to do. So as I waited for my day in court, I couldn't help thinking, what had I done that was so very wrong that my life could come to this?

Part two

Tehran to Thames Valley

1 **Becoming British**

My father always wore his police uniform. Wherever we went, even to the cinema in the evening, he was always a policeman. In Iran, he said, being a policeman was something to be proud of. People gave the police respect. It was a job that carried status, and your job didn't vanish just because your shift had finished.

I was born in 1962, in Tehran; my brother Hamid is one year younger than me. When I was four years old, my parents divorced, and after that I was brought up by my father and his parents. I grew up among policemen: my grandfather had been the assistant commissioner of police, and my uncles were in the force too. By the time I was four years old I wanted to be a policeman like they were.

My father wasn't so sure. He wanted me to make the sort of money that his friends who were doctors or lawyers could make. Although my dad was the head of the Tehran traffic police, we were not well off. When we were young, we used to visit the much bigger houses of other policemen that my father knew.

'Why do they have swimming pools, and we don't?' I would ask him, disappointed.

He didn't tell me that those colleagues got a swimming pool by taking backhanders. Much later, after the Iranian revolution, many of them paid for their corrupt activities with their lives. 'Their swimming pools came back to haunt them,' my father would say. For six years before I was born he had worked for the Iranian police anti-corruption group, hundreds of miles away in the south of the country, and he knew the temptations that police officers faced. Having investigated them, he also knew the potential cost of giving in to temptation.

Queen Elizabeth II had visited Iran in 1961, and as a traffic cop, my father had escorted her. Prince Philip had commended him, which made him – still makes him – very proud. When we were young, my father decided that Hamid and I would have a better chance of becoming successful if we were educated in England.

He had visited England several times, for a holiday. 'Everything is there,' he told us, while he looked for a suitable boarding school to make us into doctors or lawyers. Any school at that time would have had its work cut out to turn me into anything useful. Despite my father's strict house rules, and the punishments if I didn't do my homework, I was a poor student. It didn't look as if I would fulfil his ambitions if I stayed in Tehran.

We were not poor, but he certainly didn't have enough money to send us halfway round the world to boarding school, so he took extra jobs. At the weekend, he became a second-hand car dealer, buying and selling to supplement his salary. Some of the money he invested in a taxi, which he leased out during the week for a cut of the takings. Combining all his money-making schemes, he could scrape together the school fees, the cost of our school uniforms and flights, and enough for 25 pence a week pocket money each while we were there.

In August 1972 Hamid and I boarded a flight from Tehran to London. My father, in his uniform, walked right on to the plane with us, although he wasn't coming. On the same flight was the Iranian weightlifting team, so he took the coach to one side and ordered him to look after us until we reached Amsterdam, where we were changing flights. There was the small problem that we didn't know what to do after the weightlifters had left us. In 1972 airports didn't have trained staff to accompany kids through the corridors – and we didn't speak Dutch. We could say 'thank you' in English, and nothing else. In Iran we speak Farsi, which is written in the Arabic alphabet, so we couldn't even try to make out the signs in the airport.

'Just follow everyone else' was my father's advice. In Amsterdam, we did that, and almost got out of the airport before someone spotted that we were about to miss our connecting flight.

My father had remarried, and my stepmother, whose family lived in Highgate in North London, was there to meet us at Heathrow airport. England looked, sounded and smelt different. Looking out of the car window, I had never even seen yellow street lights before; as a culture shock this was pretty minor compared to the next morning, when Hamid and I were served with our first English breakfast of fried egg, bacon, sausage and baked beans. This was a strange country where people didn't eat bread and cheese in the morning.

After breakfast, to the car: it was time to start our new life. The school my father had chosen is called Slindon College. It is south of London, near the south coast, nestled among traditional English towns like Bognor Regis, Arundel and Chichester. It's a small school – today it has around 100 pupils – and the boarders live in an old Tudor-period manor house, which to us looked like a giant, evil castle.

But my father had got his dates wrong, and we were one month early for the start of term. We had arrived right in the middle of the summer holiday. There was no one there but Mr Wright, the headmaster, who approached the Iranian family climbing out of the car at the end of his long driveway in a state of some confusion, surrounded by a pack of pet whippets. I had never seen such skinny dogs.

'If that's how he starves dogs,' I thought, 'what's he going to do to us?'

It was decided that we were staying. A £10 note for each of us from my stepmother, and they were gone. Hamid and I sat down in the deserted tennis courts, and cried. We weren't going to see our father for years, we had no idea what anyone was saying, no friends and nothing to do. I had made my father promise that if I agreed to go to school in England he would buy me a motorbike. I had looked for it that morning with no success, and being stuck miles from anywhere in a strange country where we weren't even wanted wasn't making me feel better.

We explored: there were baths, but no showers. How would we wash? In Iran, we had been taught that baths were unhygienic, because you sit in pools of lukewarm dirty water. Were English people this dirty? These baths were old, and stained through years of use. The toilets were a mystery too: in Tehran, after you went to the toilet you washed yourself clean. In Slindon College, you used toilet paper, which we had never seen. We were given food we didn't recognise and didn't know how to eat. For pudding, we had sponge pudding with thick yellow goo on it. This, we discovered, was custard. I was already counting the days until I could go back to civilisation.

Our induction was helped by a local Iranian who would sometimes come and visit us, and teach us a little English. We would tell him that they weren't feeding us enough, and we would end up like the whippets, so he taught us to go back to the serving hatch, and say, 'More, please', like two Iranian Oliver Twists. But he couldn't prepare us for the biggest shock of all: our new friends.

When you are smaller than the other kids, when you don't speak the language, when you don't have pocket money and your father is thousands of miles away, a British boarding school is not the place you want to be. For the first two years, it often felt as if we had been sent to prison. British public schoolboys can be creative and dedicated bullies – I can't count the number of times my head was flushed down the toilet. The older children liked to use me as a sort of slave: Lawford dressed like a 1950s rocker, and made me clean his room and make his bed for him. Vincent was more of a hippy, so I had to walk to the village to buy his cigarettes for him instead, and Addul was a Saudi prince who apparently had a real gun – and so everyone, me included, was scared of him. It could have been worse – unlike some of the rich kids, my pocket money didn't stretch to funding Vincent's habit, so he reluctantly gave me money to buy cigarettes. Everyone called me 'Fuzzball', because of the blob of thick, curly hair on my head. Every night in Becket junior dormitory, I would cringe with embarrassment as I had to get undressed in front of ten other kids. It didn't help that, as I could hardly speak, read or write in English and wasn't physically strong, I wasn't really good at anything.

And like in prison, if you are the weakling at a British boarding school you can't rely on the staff to take care of you all the time. You have to find some way to prove yourself, and at Slindon a kid called Kevin Cheshire saved me. He was one of my few friends, and one of the school's high achievers. He did it by working hard, every day and every evening. It wasn't glamorous or easy, but I copied everything he did, and my grades began to improve slowly. English was always a problem, but I managed B grades in two English O level exams at sixteen, and passed six other subjects. With puberty I filled out, and turned from one of the smallest kids into one of the largest. I discovered a talent for rugby, and eventually captained the school team, playing as a tough number eight, and was selected for West Sussex, the county side.

My other mentor was a teacher, who is still teaching at Slindon today. Nick Pinney was a tough Welsh rugby coach and geography teacher, and he toughened me up, showed me how to stand up to bullies. In a few years, I went from being a little, mute Iranian kid to being house captain. I was sometimes invited to have dinner with the headmaster and his guests, and instead of picking on me, the other kids tended to look to me when they wanted someone who would stand up to the teachers and ask for something, whether it was an extra hour at the local disco on

Saturday, or more food (a recurring theme), or just the chance to watch *Top of the Pops* on TV. I was their unofficial advocate.

I had also turned into a bit of a bastard. There is not much opportunity to be nice at boarding school, and I became a product of the system. I had not risen above the mild brutality of boarding school life, I just got a better deal from it. Having to fight for everything means that you learn to fight for anything, and I developed a habit of pushing the rules as far as they could go, playing the system for what we could get. It wasn't a fun place to be, but it taught me some useful lessons: on the good side, it taught me to stand up for what I believe in, that people respect achievement, and that you can beat bullies. On the other hand, I realised later that life should be about more than being the strongest, and using your strength to crush others. Other kids at Slindon didn't do as well out of the system as I did, and they needed someone to look out for them, just as I had needed someone to look out for me in my early years.

One thing boarding school teaches you early: independence. As I reached the sixth form, that was to become the most valuable lesson of all, because my entry to the sixth form coincided with the revolution in Iran. At the beginning of 1979, the Shah left for France, Ayatollah Khomeini returned from exile, and soon Iran had been declared an Islamic state, with a new, far stricter government and a crackdown on the figureheads of the old regime. We were worried about our father, who had been influential under the Shah. When we finally reached him on the phone, he told us not to worry. He had been promoted. Most of the officers above him had mysteriously disappeared, so for a little while, he was acting head of police. The corruption of the previous regime had given his superiors a grand lifestyle with their own swimming pools, but his reputation for honesty and straight dealing had literally saved his life.

It was the end of our time at Slindon though, because father could not send money out of the country to pay the bills. Even today, it is hard to send money back to friends and relatives inside Iran, or for them to send money out.

We had one month to find alternative accommodation, so we went to live in a hotel.

This wasn't luxury: one of my father's friends ran a small tourist hotel in Gloucester Road, in West London. He let us live in one room while we tried to sort out our next step, lending me enough money to enrol at the Modern Tutorial College in Kilburn to study for a single A level, instead of the three I would have been taking. After a few weeks my father's friend needed the room, so for several months we were passed between relatives and friends: a few weeks here, a few weeks there. No one knew what to do with us. We couldn't go home to Iran, and there was nowhere for us in London.

Hamid and I found jobs working in one of West London's Iranian restaurants. West London is home to around 40,000 Iranians, some of whom I was to meet again later when the area became part of my operational command. In 1979, I started at the bottom. I was a waiter, and Hamid washed dishes for 90 pence an hour, cash in hand.

Getting a job meant we could find somewhere to live. We found a room in Ladbroke Grove, now a well-off area, but then a run-down locality, and a traditional destination for London's immigrants for thirty years. We lived above a butcher's shop – you got to the room by walking through his shop, with its strong smell of raw meat. It would have been an exciting smell for some of the other visitors, who were popping into the brothel on the floor above us. When we were not working, we used to sit in our room, from where we could see the customers come and go on the stairs outside our door. Once, inspired by the crime fighters in our favourite cop show, *The Professionals*, I made my first amateur arrest. A punter came running down the stairs – he had skipped out without paying. He thought he had made a clean getaway, until he was floored by what he thought were two young pimps. It was Hamid and me; and at the time, it seemed about as close as I was going to get to being a police officer.

School had taught me the value of working your way out of a problem, piece by piece. Sandwiched in our single room with butchers below and whores above, chased home at night by skinheads who called me a Paki, I still wanted to get my education. I wanted to be a policeman, but I didn't want to spend my life frustrated in my job by my lack of education. So I lied my way on to a Higher National Diploma course at South West London College of Business Education by telling them that I had management experience at the restaurant, which would have been quite a surprise to the owner had they checked. University was out of the question with one A level in biology, but I could study for a vocational course, an HND in business management. Work was looking up too, with a job in Pizza Hut, manning the ovens. I was insanely competitive. If I couldn't go to university, I wanted to be the best 'oven man' in Pizza Hut instead. My arms were notched with the oven burns that I acquired every Friday and Saturday night, when the restaurants were full and only a good oven man could stop the pizzas from burning.

I would finish my HND course in Brixton at 5 pm, and my shift started in Harrow an hour later. It's a seventeen-mile journey through the centre of London, so the only way to make it was to buy a motorbike and dash through the rush-hour traffic. During quiet periods at work, I would stop watching the pizza ovens and do my homework. Work finished at 1 am, and I would be back in Ladbroke Grove by 2 am. We didn't become as thin as the whippets, because there were always leftovers. Hamid brought home kebabs from the Iranian restaurant where he worked, and I brought back pizza.

I was doing well in my course, but I still struggled with my written English; nevertheless when I got a distinction in my

HND course, it meant I could skip the first year of a law degree when I was accepted at London's City University Law School in 1982. I still wanted to be a cop, although I didn't tell my father, who was still in Tehran. He was pleased that his son would be able to become a lawyer, and repay the investment he had made to send me away to study.

I desperately wanted to show everyone that I was as good as they were. At times it was comic. Hamid and I pooled all our savings, ran up our credit cards to the limit and worked extra shifts to buy a car. We didn't want any car: we bought a BMW 320i, black, customised with a rear spoiler and skirting. One day I was watching the ridiculous TV show *Knight Rider*, in which the hero David Hasselhoff drives a car that talks to him and helps him catch the bad guys. The car had a set of tiny lights on the front that blinked from right to left and back again. I had to have something like it, and after badgering a mechanic into doing me a cut-price deal, I did.

I was flash, I was cool, I must have made some people laugh their heads off when I drove to my lectures on the one day a week that I could actually afford petrol to put into the car.

'Never show weakness,' I would tell myself. Sometimes that would help. Other times, my desire never to take a backward step would land me in trouble.

When I was prosecuted for careless driving after pulling my beautiful BMW out of a junction in front of someone, I wasn't going to show weakness. Instead of accepting the three points on my licence and pleading guilty, I insisted on a trial at Ealing Magistrates' Court, at which I was to use all of my legal experience to defend myself.

'You're mad,' my friends told me, but I wouldn't listen. I insisted on cross-examining the police officers at the scene, and brought forward precedents where the House of Lords had ruled on the exact legal definition of the word 'careless'. It was a

stunning failure. I got three penalty points, and quite rightly had
to pay £100 costs for wasting everyone's time.

Underneath, I was trying to fast-forward my life: to act like the
successful guy that I wasn't yet, whose major achievement outside
academic life was acquiring a solid reputation for cooking pizza
well. So it was no surprise that in my second year, I squeezed in
marriage too, to a woman I had known for a month, who didn't
even live in London.

Sally and I met when I went with a few of my friends to the
Isle of Wight for a holiday: she was one of the locals. A month
later, I popped back with a couple of witnesses and we went to
the local register office. It was an informal wedding; I wore jeans
for it. My father wasn't there, because I didn't tell him about it,
knowing that he would disapprove. I went back to London to
carry on studying for my degree, and Sally stayed on the island
she had never left in her life, with a vague idea that we would be
together soon.

Combining a degree with work, rugby, marriage and maintaining
a BMW got me a lower second in my final exams – respectable,
but I should have done better. By now, I was creating a fantasy
life for my father, who thought I was a single, soon-to-be lawyer.
He was delighted when I decided to train as a barrister, so that I
could argue cases in court.

I joined the one-year course offered by the Inns of Court School
of Law. In the UK, to be a barrister, you need to be a member of
one of the four Inns of Court, which date back hundreds of years
to the beginning of British common law. The school was set up
by the Inns to train lawyers to become barristers.

I had a different motivation: I wanted it to train me to become
a better police officer. In the British army, you can either join as
a private, at the lowest level, or if you pass an assessment and
training, join as an officer, and reach the highest ranks if your
ability takes you there. Not so in the police: everyone joins as

a constable, the 'bobby on the beat', and gains experience of everyday policing before they have the opportunity to command other officers. It has advantages and disadvantages. In its favour, every serving policeman in the UK knows what it is like to patrol the streets as a constable. They know the everyday problems and frustrations, and have experienced the camaraderie of the force.

On the other hand, it's important to spot talent early, and make sure that anyone who has potential can rise through the ranks relatively early in their career. There's little point in talented and ambitious officers gaining responsibility just before they retire, when their experience of day-to-day policing may be twenty years out of date. That is why there is an Accelerated Promotion Course for new entrants to the police force who show potential to reach the highest ranks.

I guessed it would be tough competing with others who were born and bred here and perhaps had more contacts than me. I wanted to guarantee I would get on that course, and that meant being overqualified to be a police constable.

But at the Inns of Court I was out of my depth. The training was tough, and I struggled – making an argument in front of a judge is hard to do, and I was conscious that I didn't have the education that many of the others did. A lot of them cherished a career at the bar in the same way that I had ambitions only to be a policeman, and had been preparing for this course for years. They also had the confidence of people who were born to be barristers in the English legal system. They had completed a public school education, few would have paid for college by baking pizzas, and none would have lived under a brothel. Some were educated at Oxford and Cambridge, and knew how to handle the confusing formal dinners, where we wore formal gowns and made small talk at long tables.

I didn't know any small talk. Networking was excruciating. It was like being eight years old. I was scared and mute.

I dreaded the drinks parties, where I was introduced to

judges with whom I had nothing in common, and was expected to make an impression. My classmates were much better than me at making good impressions. In 1986 there were not many black and Asian law students who wanted to be barristers. We stuck out. This was my first exposure to what Brits call 'the Establishment' – the informal group of senior, powerful people from whom the leaders of government and industry are chosen. The Establishment has its own unwritten customs and rules, some of which are obvious, some of which are intimidating to outsiders, and some of which you only know about when you break them. The Establishment has a set of common interests and expectations, which I could fake, to a point. After all, I had been to boarding school, so I wasn't completely naive. Crucially though, the Establishment values its common background. I felt that I was forever disqualified: being Iranian – a Muslim – wasn't the best start. Having a single A level in biology doesn't demonstrate the right credentials, and an HND is rarely the sign of what they might call 'a first-class mind'.

Many people with HNDs don't have what it takes to be a successful barrister, and I might well have failed if that is the route I had wanted to take, but that is hardly the point. Organisations where the leaders recruit only people who share their values often miss out on the diversity of talent available from people who have taken a different route to the same destination and don't necessarily share the same background and system of values. These monolithic organisations can be comfortable places to work because everyone identifies with each other, and so there is not much internal conflict; but they are rarely the best at providing a service to their customers. The bar in 1986 was not a welcoming place for people like me.

It was no surprise to me that, ultimately, I failed to make it as a barrister: during your training, you endlessly visit the firms (known as chambers) of barristers clustered around London's law courts, looking for a pupillage – that is, to be taken on for no salary as the most junior member of the chambers. My patchy résumé wasn't up to it, and I didn't make a good impression. I received no offers.

One day I found a piece of paper listing names of chambers that had been left in the canteen of the Bar Council. Whoever had left it behind had highlighted one name and written beside it: 'Uncle Freddie. Must apply.' Another address had 'Dad's friend – speak to him before applying.'

It was time to upset my father, and be honest about what I really wanted to do. I applied to join the police.

2 In uniform

'Whitley? I didn't think they had police houses in Whitley.'

Fresh out of my police training course, I had just met the man who was going to introduce me to the job, and already he thought I was a joke. With a law degree, a public school education and a brown face, I tended to stick out from the crowd during the fifteen-week training course I had just finished. Now my mentor, known as a 'constable tutor' in the police, would guide me through my probation: a time when I would make the jump from the classroom and parade ground in Cwymbran, South Wales, to the streets of Reading, in the Thames Valley.

My tubby, chain-smoking constable tutor was impressed by my uselessness. 'You'll go a long way in the police,' he told me, 'because you have no common sense.'

If he thought I was funny, at least I could have a laugh at his expense in return. His name was Constable Mick Constable.

Constable Constable wasn't the only person in my life who thought I had made the wrong decision. My father pointed out to me that he hadn't paid for nine years of private education so that I could walk the beat as PC Dizaei. His view was confirmed when he saw the police house in which I would live, and I discovered what Constable Constable was talking about. Overall, Reading is one of the best-off areas in Britain. Gross weekly pay is about 20 per cent higher than the national average, and a detached house sells for 43 per cent more.

But this disguises pockets of poverty and crime. The most

significant is the Whitley estate, built in the 1930s to replace a local slum near a sewage works which gives rise to what Reading's residents call the 'Whitley whiff'. Despite initiatives to help the residents of the area, Thames Valley Police still describes Whitley as 'complex' to police, to this day. For example, in 2004, bus drivers threatened not to go to the estate after several buses were pelted with stones and shotgun pellets. One bus driver had ammonia thrown in his face. Kids have always used the streets of Whitley to race stolen cars, which they then set alight. Whitley is the heartland of support for the far-right British National Party in Reading. 'We are the good people,' said the BNP Reading spokesman Dr Phil Edwards in 2003. 'Multi-culturalism isn't doing us any good. All it has given us is chicken tikka masala and a few good footballers.' Overall, the Reading area has twice as many burglaries per head of population as the rest of the country (in 2003, 14.5 per 1,000 people compared to the national average of 6.7) and your car is twice as likely to be stolen (9.7 thefts per 1,000 people, compared to 4.8).

Fourteen other Thames Valley probationer constables joined at the same time as me, all white-skinned. I was the one who got a police house in the BNP heartland of Hartland Road, Whitley. Multi-culturalism had given Whitley one more gift it didn't like: me. I was an Iranian immigrant and a copper – and in Whitley that was like being black twice over.

While I was in Cwymbrn, my first wife and I divorced. We never had to separate, because we never lived together for more than a few weeks, but I had met Natalie, a nurse, who had treated me for an injury to my collar bone that I picked up playing rugby. We were married in Ealing register office; this time my father knew all about it, and was there for the wedding. My new wife, my brother and I had moved up in the world: we were already renting a small flat in Ealing, and now I was being provided with my first house.

My father and I packed up my belongings, and shipped them

to my new house in Whitley. The gate had been pulled off the hinges, and was gone. Rubbish was piled up in the garden. Inside, the last inhabitants had been squatters, who had helpfully lit a fire in the front room – in the middle of the floor. I soon found out that they weren't absolutely the last inhabitants, as the house was infested with rats. The house was, by any standards, derelict.

It took four days for my father, my brother and me to clean it up to the point where I could live in it; bringing Natalie to live with me wasn't an option. The local environmental health department put down poison to kill the rats. For nine months, this was to be my home. I bought some homing pigeons like the ones I had kept in Iran as a boy, to give me something to do, and kept them in a shed in the garden. One night, the local kids broke into the shed and stole them as a prank. They obviously weren't master criminals, as three days later, the homing pigeons returned, just like they were trained to do.

I was upset, but not nearly as upset as when I came home one night and found 'Pakis out of Britain' painted on my front door. It was then that I bought a big dog, a Doberman, to keep me company.

By this stage, there was one other police resident of the Whitley estate: Denzil Macintosh was in the probation class after me, and we had struck up a friendship. Denzil was an ex-Jamaican police officer who had decided to commence employment with Thames Valley Police and was a little nervous of being housed in Whitley. His wife wasn't crazy about living in Whitley either, especially when local residents shat in a jam jar and threw it through their bedroom window while they slept. Denzil and I had a lot in common. We were the only two probationer constables in Whitley. We were both in houses that were barely habitable. We were the only two probationers in Reading who weren't white, and for some reason, we had been put in the area where we were absolutely guaranteed to be resented, threatened and abused.

Perhaps this assignment, probably a little joke from the person who allocated the police housing, was a way to toughen us up for life in the police. I had quickly discovered that when I joined the police my colour was a daily topic of comment, much of it abusive, for other people both inside and outside the force. As a trainee barrister, I felt an outsider because I didn't have the education or the smoothness to fit in. In the police, as on the Whitley estate, the problem was more basic: I was, in the description used around the station house, a Paki.

At Cwymbrn, the drill sergeant instructing us had a funny joke for me when he heard I was of Iranian origin. In a tribute to the violence of the Iranian revolution – which had also inspired my nickname of 'Ayatollah' – whenever he saw me, he would mime unclipping and throwing a grenade in my direction. When I was chatting to the other trainees, they would joke that the bad odour they could smell must be me, because I had been eating curry. More sinister, there was a general assumption that blacks and Asians who weren't up to the job were being let into the force: political correctness meant that black and Asian recruits could fail their exams – we took one a week – and still pass. I didn't help by failing my first exam, which was doubly embarrassing, because it was a multiple-choice test about British law.

There was no incident that, by itself, was serious enough to make me accuse anyone of racism, but I felt singled out, different, an outsider looking in. For a while, I laughed along in this strange new environment, where my colour had suddenly become the single most important thing about me. After a few weeks, I realised that the jokes weren't going to go away. If I was going to stick it out, it would be hard to ever simply be 'one of the lads'.

I had been expecting some resentment from some people outside the force. I wasn't stupid: no one is going to thank you for arresting them, and my colour was an obvious focus for the abuse I would get. But I genuinely hadn't expected the level of hostility I got from my new colleagues. After three weeks of the fifteen-week course, I nearly quit because of it, but at the last minute I decided to stick it out.

Almost a year later, working my shift in Reading, I had reached the end of my tether. I had been living in a slum for nine months. I was doing well at the job, but I resented the fact that Denzil and I were a two-man ghetto, suffering daily racist abuse, living in fear. I wanted to fit in. I was keenly aware that as a probationer, I could be dismissed at any time, and I didn't want to make a fuss, but no one was listening to my complaints. So I decided to go to see Chief Superintendent Lord.

The chief superintendent runs your police station. He's your boss. Between him and me there were constables, sergeants, inspectors, chief inspectors and superintendents. He would not have expected to speak to me, and I had no reasonable expectation that I would speak to him, except that my complaint wasn't the usual probationer moaning.

If rank-and-file officers have had a problem with racism, then that gives the senior ranks a problem too, because they have to try and resolve that problem. Race problems have a deserved reputation for being difficult to handle and sensitive, not least because the police force does not look like the rest of the population. Today, just as in 1986, there simply aren't enough black or Asian police officers. The police have never recruited their fair share of officers from the non-white population, and when they recruit, they don't retain enough. The efforts by senior ranks to make the police more attractive to non-whites had led, in the minds of my fellow probationers, to all sorts of preferential treatment for black and Asian recruits. On the other hand, the opinion among the black and Asian community was completely the opposite: that often non-white police officers were discriminated against, and would have to try twice as hard for recognition. Most senior officers have tried hard to dispel both points of view, with limited success.

I could have turned into just one more black PC who

dropped out of the force. Instead, I decided to fight. Eventually I summoned the courage to complain that after the best part of a year the racial abuse I was receiving in my house hadn't stopped, and that despite my best efforts to repair my house I was still living under siege, as was Denzil. Chief Supt Lord's secretary certainly didn't think that a complaint about poor housing for two probationers was worth bothering her boss about. 'If you have a problem, go and see your sergeant,' she told me when I asked to see him in late 1986.

'I'd prefer to see the chief superintendent,' I said. 'It's about racism.'

'Ah. When would you like an appointment?' she said.

Chief Supt Lord sucked his pipe as I told him about the writing on my front door.

'We'll get the patrols round your area a bit more,' he said, without taking the pipe out of his mouth.

I told him about the state of the building. He promised to get some decorators in.

'We are the only two black probationers in Thames Valley Police,' I told him. 'None of the white probationers were sent to Whitley.' That got the pipe out of his mouth. He promised to send one of his inspectors around to inspect the house, who reported that he wouldn't house a dog where I was living. Denzil and I were rehoused. My house was put up for sale, and Thames Valley Police decided not to house police officers on the Whitley estate in future.

This little confrontation had set a pattern that was going to be repeated for many years. When I thought I was getting an unfair deal, I would stick up for myself. Sometimes I got a fair hearing, and sometimes I didn't. Inevitably the complaints were often about racism. I was, in the opinion of one fellow officer, 'obsessed with race'. I wasn't, I was obsessed with being given what I was due, when I had earned it. I didn't want preferential treatment – I wanted what others accepted as their right. I have never 'played the race card' – that is, I have never used the colour of my skin to ask for special treatment.

It was hard not to be 'obsessed with race' on the beat in Reading, when a fellow PC tells you out of the blue that he has 'just seen your wife walking up Hartland Road with a monkey under her arm.' The 'monkey' he was talking about was my new baby. He was supposed to be my friend, someone I could rely on, but I would often find that race hate was a daily topic of conversation in the police force.

I admit it: I do have an obsession. I want everyone to get what they deserve. That means black people, white people, rich people and poor people, innocent people who deserve protection and criminals who deserve punishment. It was a lesson I learnt from PC Constable during my probation – by learning to do everything that he didn't do.

PC Constable was, even in 1986, a dinosaur who reflected the old police force. If you wanted to be generous, you would call him 'streetwise'. He was dedicated to doing as little as possible, but he was always anxious to teach me a life lesson. One of my first nights on duty, I followed him down to a club near Reading station, then called Sloppy Joe's – a notorious trouble spot. He chatted to the owner for a couple of minutes as we stood at the bar. Two pints of lager appeared.

'Get that down your neck,' he said.

I said to him that we couldn't drink, we were on duty. He looked at me as if I was speaking Farsi, hardly able to believe what he was hearing. It was probably the most ridiculous thing he'd ever heard from a probationer.

'Anyway,' I added, 'I don't drink.' No, that was it.

PC Constable taught me the first lesson of my probation.

'The first thing you learn is to do as you're told,' he said. I took a tiny sip, and chewed gum for the rest of my shift in case anyone could smell alcohol on me.

The other lessons he tried to pass on were mostly about economy of effort, or in police slang, 'coughing the job'. It's a phrase that's used to describe officers who avoid work as much as possible by doing as little as possible, encouraging people not to report crimes, cutting any corner to avoid paperwork or legwork. PC Constable was the most dedicated cougher I have seen. Lesson two came when we found an Asian minicab driver by the road one night. His nose and left eye were bleeding after one of his passengers had attacked him. He was, not surprisingly, upset, and started to tell my tutor what had happened.

'Hang on a minute,' said PC Constable, and unzipped his fly. Without pausing to stub out his cigarette, he started to urinate on the roadside while listening to the taxi driver's story. Mick Constable had many faults, but this showed that he knew how to multitask.

For him, disposing of this case was as easy as zipping up his fly. 'It happens, OK?' he told the stunned taxi driver. 'Go on your way.'

In a moment, we were saved the chore of taking him to a hospital, taking a statement from him, conducting house-to-house searches for witnesses, or visiting the taxi office to get a description of the passenger. We were spared the tedium of attempting to make an arrest, and the time and expense of perhaps prosecuting the assailant, with all the paperwork it would have involved. The only cost to us, shamefully, was ignoring a crime against someone who needed our protection more than most.

Mick Constable's lesson three was the scariest for me personally: never overreact. Early in my probation, we were called to a domestic dispute. A father and son were arguing with each other. When we arrived, I turned out to be the perfect distraction, because as soon as he saw me, the son forgot the argument with his father. He had someone he could hate more.

'You Paki bastard,' he said, 'I'm going to get you.'

'Mick!' I said. 'Do I arrest him?' At that moment, PC Constable was busy smoking. He weighed up the situation.

'He's only kidding,' he said.

The son went inside to get a carving knife, and brought it out.

'Mick!' I said. 'What do I do?'

'Don't overreact,' he said.

The son waggled the knife at me.

'Mick!' I wailed, trying not to overreact, as instructed.

'Leave him,' said the father to his son, 'he hasn't done anything to you.'

This, like Mick's policy of non-intervention, didn't seem to help. It spurred the son into lunging at me with his carving knife. At this moment, I realised that Constable Constable's tuition was about to make my police career a short one. This was perhaps the moment to take the initiative and do things my way.

'Fuck you, Mick!' I shouted, pulled out my truncheon and hit the guy on the head, which wasn't where we were supposed to hit anyone, but was the only bit of him I could be sure to hit in my panic. The guy missed me, and gave me a chance to grab the knife. After forty-five minutes of struggle, we finally had him in handcuffs – thankfully his father had supported me. I had made a decision. From now on, there would be no coughing the job.

3 Them and us

It's December 1986. I'm standing in a line, under a helmet, in the middle of the countryside. On either side of me, other Thames Valley constables are linked together. It's cold, it's wet, and we're trying to stop people from throwing themselves under lorries. A bag filled with urine sails through the air towards me; I spot it at the last minute and dodge to one side. My mate's not so lucky. It hits him square in the face and bursts open.

Today it's urine. A few weeks ago, they threw tampons at us instead. Welcome to the Greenham Common protests: four months previously, my evenings at the Inns of Court had been spent at formal candlelit dinners, where a professional mistake was using the wrong fork.

In 1986, Greenham Common was the focus of protests against nuclear weapons being based on British soil. Since 14 November 1983, nuclear missiles had been stationed at the US air base there, creating a rallying point for thousands of protesters who had established a peace camp there. The camp was inhabited almost exclusively by women, and in 1982 9,000 women had linked hands and surrounded the air base in a peaceful protest.

By 1986, the protests were a lot nastier. Protesters took to blocking traffic going in and out of the base by sitting in the road and singing songs. It was an effective tactic which attracted a lot of attention in the press, who took opposing views: to some, the Greenham women were heroes. To others, they were dangerous left-wing subversives.

It wasn't the job of the police officers of Thames Valley Police to make those distinctions. Sitting in the road to block the traffic was against the law. We pledged to uphold the law. That meant we had to try and clear the roads – often by arresting the protesters who wouldn't move. On one night alone, we arrested more than fifty women. It was horrible work, and a bag of urine in the face didn't improve it.

On the other hand, if you are a dedicated police officer, it is also thrilling. You are doing a difficult job, one which most people would shirk. You bond with your mates, rely on each other in a situation that's a million miles away from the drudgery of doing paperwork or manning a desk. If you don't do your job, then your colleagues are in real danger. Whether it's policing a football match, making an arrest of a dangerous suspect, chasing a criminal in a car or walking into the middle of a fight in a pub, as a police officer you trust your colleagues to back you up, and know that you would back them up too. That's partly why the police have their own culture, why they see themselves as a close unit, why they tend to stick together out of work too. It's known as the 'canteen culture' – a shared set of opinions, based on day-to-day life, that forges close bonds in the face of a dangerous job where on any day you might get injured or killed. Firefighters have a similar culture. Even the rugby teams I played for have a similar set of bonds.

The police couldn't function without the camaraderie that creates a team with a common goal out of a group of individuals. Yet that culture also has its dark side.

It's inevitable that in creating a close-knit team, that team develops a common mindset, and in the police, that mindset could be described as 'them and us'. You're either on our side, or you're against us. It doesn't help that as a police officer, 80 per cent of your shift is spent interacting with people who are giving you problems. They don't like you; you're trying to stop them from doing something. Eventually, you begin to think that everyone you meet shares the same view – you're sensitive to it, waiting for trouble. The 'them' becomes anyone who doesn't share your view of the world.

So what defines the 'us'? There has been a lot of research done into how police officers, especially the lower ranks, see the world. One of the most important books on the subject was written by Professor Simon Holdaway in 1983. *Inside the British Police* was researched during his eleven years as a serving police officer. He did the research by listening to and recording what his own colleagues said. Today, he is head of the school of law at the University of Sheffield, a consultant to the National Police Training Development Unit, and was consulted by the British government when they were preparing research on the future of a multi-ethnic Britain. In 1983, he was Sergeant Holdaway.

The book describes how his fellow officers had their own 'occupational culture' – the way in which they took the rules and regulations of policing, and moderated them to fit their shared view of the outside world. Because the ordinary ranks of the police force – four out of five police officers in the UK are constables, the lowest rank – have a lot of discretion in how they apply the law, this meant that often the occupational culture was more significant in deciding how the police responded to a situation than the regulations and policies applied by the top 1 per cent who were at the rank of superintendent or above.

At one point he relates a conversation with a senior officer. 'Policemen must be willing to cut corners or they would never get the job done. Secondly, it's because policemen have been willing to gild the lily that the law gets administered in this country.'

That's the most important point about 'them' and 'us' – you don't find a definition written down in any set of guidelines. There's a difference between police policy in action, and police policy as it is written.

He also relates how the further the officers were from their 'ground' – the police station – the more vulnerable they felt. They 'perceive the local population as part of a world potentially erupting into disorder – the police save it from sliding over the edge.'

Point two – the public needs 'us' to protect it from an imminent danger from 'them'. It's understandable for police officers to feel constantly under attack. In some situations, like at Greenham Common, they are. They receive heavy criticism from some groups for doing their job, when often there is no practical alternative. Maintaining law and order isn't always an easy job, but someone has to do it, and when you do a good, professional job and still receive criticism, that fosters resentment.

Most strikingly, Holdaway also saw how this leads to a tendency to label other people doing their job as a threat to the police's effort to maintain that order. Among the threats Holdaway described were doctors, who could allege that a prisoner had been mistreated; solicitors, who would use legal tricks to get guilty criminals off the hook and make the police look bad; and women, who sometimes didn't share the view that the world was divided into 'good' and 'bad' in the same way. Each of these groups was routinely criticised, caricatured and abused in the station house, behind the scenes.

So point three is, you don't have to be a criminal to be 'not one of us'. You just have to be seen to criticise the occupational police culture.

In later years, Holdaway has done a lot of work on race and the police, and has concluded that the occupational culture can often be racist. He wrote in a paper called 'Police Race Relations' that 'Stereotyping, banter and a stress on membership of a tightly-knit team of officers have been found to reinforce negative classification of minority police officers' and 'The occupational culture has specific features that marginalise members of minorities within the workforce.' His conclusion is that, unless this is tackled, the British police tends to welcome ethnic minority recruits through the front door formally, and informally encourages them to leave through the back door.

In other words, in the canteen culture, blacks aren't the only enemy; but being black marks you out as potentially not 'one of us', and sometimes your fellow officers will act as if you are as much an enemy as the criminals they are trying to stop.

This doesn't mean that every day in the police is a living hell; far from it. While I was made aware of my race every day, often this was harmless, even quite funny. One of my best friends in the force, and still a friend today, was PC Albert Bernard. Black, 6 ft 5 in tall, he was an imposing figure, which was handy because his beat was Coley Park in Reading, the only area that could compete with the neighbouring Whitley estate for crime. For a while we shared a beat, arriving in our police car at the scene of the many night-time disturbances in the area. In the station we were known as the 'ethnic response unit'.

When the joking got nasty, it was hard to handle. I could take the abuse from the public – I had grown up with it in my flat above the butcher's shop. But I wasn't paid extra to take the abuse from my own colleagues, and one day, I snapped.

I was still a probationer when a group of us were waiting in a police van, on football duty. It's one of the high-pressure situations where you feel under threat. You have nothing to do except wait to be called on, you're itching to get out of the cramped van. When you are deployed, you often end up wishing you were back in the van. The banter starts. As usual, one PC started to abuse me, the Paki, and wouldn't shut up.

I'd had it with him. Grabbing him by the lapels, I squared up to him. 'Call me that one more time and I'll fucking deck you,' I said.

I wanted to smack him. 'You and me can settle this now. Outside.'

Luckily for my career, the inspector pulled us apart.

'If you can't take a joke, you shouldn't have joined,' the other guy said, after I had put him down.

The inspector took me aside, and asked me why I hadn't told him about the abuse I was getting. I told him that I was telling him now. I was sick of it.

Later, he told the entire shift that he wasn't going to stand for racist abuse on his shift: another insult and they'd be disciplined. It was a strong thing to do, and I should have been more grateful than I was. Unfortunately, it separated me from the group, who resented being told off. I wasn't 'one of us' any more among the people I needed to be part of.

A few weeks later, two inspectors called me into their office. They wanted to know more about me.

'What's your father's immigration status?' they asked. 'How can you and your brother afford a mortgage?' We had scraped together our savings to buy a house, which he lived in. I didn't like their tone of voice or the direction in which the questions were taking us, and asked the superintendent at Reading police station whether they were allowed to ask me questions like that. He took my interrogators to one side, and had a quiet word with them. Again, I should have been grateful – what did I expect him to do? Instead, I felt more like an outsider than ever.

If I couldn't naturally be part of the group, I was determined to prove myself by doing a good job: by achieving, by earning respect. I wanted to take the sergeant's exam, the first step on the promotion ladder, as soon as I had finished my two-year probation, and I started to revise in my spare time. Some of my colleagues thought I was mad and laughed at me, and I guess some of them thought I had ideas above my station. The usual pattern is to get more experience, then take the exam when you're ready to be promoted. I hadn't even become a fully-fledged constable yet, but I felt like a man on a mission, and as soon as I had finished my probation, I was entitled to take the exam.

When I took the exam, it was mission accomplished: the hours spent revising, and the days, weeks and months spent working in my spare time in the previous years, meant that I was more accustomed to taking an exam than many of my colleagues. I had found an unexpected benefit, that in learning more about the law, I was becoming a better copper on the beat as well. Out of 8,000 who took the exam nationally that year, I came in the top 200, and second in Thames Valley, the second-largest police force in the UK. I was delighted: it meant not only that I could apply for promotion, but that I was now on the fast track.

Because everyone joins the police at the lowest rank to get a solid grounding in the job, it's vital to have a scheme to pick potential high-fliers. I knew from before I joined what that scheme was and how I needed to get on it, and being in the top 200 was my ticket to the Accelerated Promotion Course. I wanted to be a leader, and although I was still a constable, that felt a little more likely. I felt as if I was going somewhere.

I knew though that I wasn't going to get anywhere until I had more experience, and more varied experience too. So I volunteered for a job that few in the force really want: I became an area beat officer in the Coley estate.

If part of the canteen culture assumes that the police are the last bulwark against chaos – that 'they' are in a constant struggle with 'us', then you start to measure achievement by your success against the enemy. It's like being in an army where your weapon is the power of arrest. It's the mark of respect to be a good 'thief taker', to make lots of arrests and solve a lot of crime.

A police force needs thief takers and the force's performance is partly measured, as it should be, on how well it solves crime and how many criminals it catches. No one else can do that job. But that's not what the police should do all the time. There has to be some element of the job that tries to prevent crime, to stop it occurring, to help to stop kids getting into trouble, or to defuse arguments before they escalate, to help people secure

their property or protect themselves. The first model of policing
is 'fire brigade' policing: you sit in a patrol car until someone
reports a crime. You go to the scene of the crime and try to sort it
out. You're responding to something that has already happened.
It's what makes headlines in the newspapers, and it's what
scriptwriters make films about. It's also what many police officers
might consider to be their *real* job.

Rapid response and effective detection might make some
potential criminals think twice, but not all of them. The police
also have a role in helping the community before a crime is
committed. We acknowledge it when we ask for 'more bobbies
on the beat', but inside the police force, it's not valued as highly
as it should be. The role of an area beat officer – now part of
what's called a 'Safer Neighbourhood Team' – is to work with
the community to help with general problems rather than solve
specific crimes. The job wasn't something that most police
officers traditionally lusted for. It is not glamorous and doesn't
have the adrenalin rush of a pursuit, and it can be a lonely job
– for example, during my time as an area beat officer, I often
didn't see the station for days. I'd choose my own hours, drive
to Coley Park, park my car outside Wilf's garage, do my job,
and drive home.

Area beat officer jobs are notoriously hard to fill. Often, officers
are press-ganged. In some cases in the past they were put on area
beats as a punishment, separated from their support network,
cast out into the community. In their 1994 book *Watching Police,
Watching Communities*, researchers Mike McConville and Dan
Shepherd asked a group of community beat officers what they
thought of the job. 'I was volunteered,' says one. 'In this job, you
are volunteered.' Another is in despair. 'Sometimes I just sit there
and think, God, I haven't nicked anyone for weeks.'

Their superior officers don't think much of the job either. 'The
bobby on the beat saying "hello" is doing nothing and with the
resource problem being what it is, we can't afford that anymore,'

one explains. The problem is exacerbated, because on the scale by which your success as a police officer is measured, you don't register. If you don't nick anyone, the reasoning goes, what are you doing with your time?

Some forces are more committed to community policing than others, and it is becoming more accepted as a way to fight crime at its source. The Met is an example. It has committed to placing a Safer Neighbourhood Team of one sergeant, two PCs and four community support officers on every ward in London. But at that time my superiors must have been surprised to see me volunteering to do the job for Coley Park.

Every Wednesday, I would set up a surgery at the community centre between 12 noon and 2 pm. Residents had complained to me that they never saw a policeman on the street among the high-rise blocks in Coley Park. It was a long way from the 'ground', and community policing in an area where hostility to the police was high wasn't considered a priority. Running the surgery made me visible to people who needed help, but didn't feel comfortable visiting the police station, because often there wasn't a crime to report – yet. Every week, ten or twelve people would bring their problem to me, to see what I could do about it. It might be a noisy neighbour, or a local dispute, or kids making a nuisance, or harassment. Sometimes I could act, other times it was my job to get other people involved – use my influence with the council, or explain the law and tell them the next steps to take.

However, I was getting a steady list of racial harassment complaints from the relatively few Asian families on the estate. I knew there was a race problem: after all, it's not every day, as a Muslim, that someone throws a pig's head into your garden, as had happened to me only a few months previously when I was living in Whitley. They trusted me to do something about it, instead of having to accept that the problem was simply part of daily life in Britain. In response, I created a racial harassment forum. I brought together the local council, the Commission for

Racial Equality, and the local community voluntary organisation, and once a month we would sit together and tackle the cases that I knew about. Previously, each organisation would pass the responsibility to the next, and blame the other when nothing was done. We changed that. It didn't cost anything, but achieved real results.

At the end of 1988, Shahin came to me: her family was being abused by a local racist gang, but it hadn't been possible to gather enough evidence to make an arrest. She needed police protection. I pushed, and managed to get the installation of covert CCTV cameras approved outside her house. On Christmas Day 1988, those cameras spotted the gang putting a petrol bomb through Shahin's door.

The community beat was incredibly satisfying, but I wanted to be a sergeant. Soon afterwards, I passed the board. On 20 January 1991, I arrived at Marlow police station, a tiny building where I would be the senior officer in charge of five constables. I was out of uniform, and Albert, who is 6 ft 5 in tall, heavily built, and black, decided to come with me on my first visit: the ethnic response unit off duty. We knocked on the door. The policeman who answered must have assumed we'd been nicked for a driving offence.

'You have to go to High Wycombe to produce driving documents,' he said.

'No mate, you don't understand,' Albert said, laughing, 'he's your new sergeant.' I will always remember the look on the face of the elderly policeman in the front counter.

Marlow was my first taste of command, but compared to the Whitley estate and Coley Park, or the other towns in the area, crime was strictly small-time stuff. I wanted something more challenging, so I spoke up, and asked to leave inside a couple of months. I was transferred to a job that would stretch me again: custody sergeant at High Wycombe.

The custody suite – the cells, in other words – at High Wycombe police station was everything that Marlow wasn't. It was certainly busy, especially on a weekend night. Instead of the lush green countryside around Marlow you lived in a bunker lit by artificial light, with no windows. Often I'd lose track of what time of day or night it was, because whether you were on the 6 am to 2 pm, the 2 pm to 10 pm or the 10 pm to 6 am shift, the view was the same. When you are in charge of the custody suite you can smell the urine, the filth, the puke. You can't slack off: every prisoner has to be checked at least every half hour – more often for more vulnerable people. You live in fear of a death in custody because you didn't do your job. You get pale because you hardly see the sun, and sometimes you get sick. I loved it.

Being a custody sergeant is one of the hardest jobs in the police force. In 1984, the Police and Criminal Evidence Act (PACE) was passed, and it defined for the first time in law how a prisoner should be treated – when they could be questioned, how this had to happen, how they were treated when they were detained. The custody sergeant was given the job of being the prisoner's 'friend'. You have to check that the prisoners have been arrested according to the law. You have to make sure they are treated fairly and humanely, and not questioned illegally. The custody suite is your responsibility, and under your control – an inspector might be senior to you, but he or she can't overrule your judgement in the custody suite. When your fellow officers want to lock someone up, they have to ask you – and you can say 'no' if you think it's not justified.

It's not a role that every sergeant would relish, but it suited me down to the ground. Having marked my card as someone who wouldn't 'fit in' for a quiet life, it gave me a chance to use my knowledge of the law in a positive way. One of the problems with being a custody sergeant that Mike McConville identified in his research is that, in the 'them and us' police culture, it is tough to be impartial, to put the law ahead of the wishes of your colleagues.

In a study of about 1,000 requests for detention, the custody sergeants he surveyed authorised 99.4 per cent of adult detentions and 99.7 per cent of requests to detain children. McConville concluded from this evidence and follow-up interviews that the position of custody sergeant was compromised: they 'readily go along with the wishes of case officers because they are emotionally committed to believing their version of events'. Group solidarity counts for more than the law: 'They will connive with the investigating officer in bending or breaking the rules', they are a 'facilitator, and not simply a doorkeeper'.

I'd like to think that never happened in my nick. It was tough at first to say 'no' to experienced officers. Sometimes they would try and push the boundaries, popping in unannounced to say, 'It's OK to have a word with…?' That was stretching the rules, and I had to tell them that I needed to know what they were going to ask, and make them write an entry in the log. With inexperienced officers, there was a different problem. In British law, you can't be arrested just for answering back to a police officer, but occasionally I'd see someone being brought in by an enthusiastic probationer who had got into an argument on the street and had arrested the citizen for obstruction.

Trouble is, you can't arrest someone for obstruction unless there's evidence that another member of the public was put in a position of fear and there was liable to be a breach of the peace. I couldn't agree to lock someone in a cell for a 'crime' which I used to call 'contempt of cop'.

Occasionally, when there was a serious disagreement, the chief inspector would storm downstairs.

'Whose fucking side are you on, Dizaei?' he would ask. But that's all he could do. He was on my turf.

In the custody suite, it was possible to earn respect and do the job right at the same time. Police culture isn't perfect, but one thing it does value is respect for someone who does the job well, and who lets you know where they stand. My year in the bunker showed me the value of knowing the law inside out; that you didn't have to cut corners to get the job done; that you could win respect by sticking to your principles and treating everyone by the rules – and that 'they' had rights as well as us.

Nevertheless, at the beginning of 1992, it was a relief to get back into the open air, back on the beat in High Wycombe. Having been a community beat officer, a sergeant in sleepy Marlow, and having lived the life of a mole in the custody suite, I hadn't been setting records for thief-taking – but one day, when I answered a call to pursue a stolen car, that was all about to change.

4 **Crusader**

Being back on the beat as a patrol sergeant in High Wycombe was a relief. My time in the custody suite had given me the opportunity to study for my MA – and write a dissertation on community policing which was eventually put to use inside Thames Valley Police – and to pass the inspector's exam. I wasn't going to get promoted yet, but when I had the right experience, I was ready.

When you're on the beat, the right experience sometimes comes your way.

In 1992, I answer a call: a kid has stolen a car, and it's coming my way. After a chase, I nick him for taking without consent. I offer to take home the teenage Asian kid who was responsible.

When I got to his house, his parents were relieved to see a police officer from a similar community. They didn't shout or scream – instead they invited me in for a meal. I sat on the floor with the father of the house, eating curry and bread, as he apologised for what his son had done. He then cuffed his son on the head.

'Tell Ali what you know!' he said. His son realised this was no time to argue, and started to tell me everything he knew about the Asian criminal gangs in the neighbourhood, especially one known as the Tutti Nungis ('holy shits').

When I came to High Wycombe, I told my bosses that I believed there were Asian gangs working in the area, who were connected to other gangs across the country. I'd heard of crimes where business cards had been left. 'You've just been visited by Paki Power,' they said.

My young informant told me the local gang was organised by a man called 'Superfly', who recruited young Pakistani kids. They stole sports cars to order, and he pointed me to the garages where the stolen cars were stripped for parts. He grassed up a burglar that he knew. He spilled the beans on the local guys who worked at the post office and stole the credit cards when they were sent in the post. He even told me which local cafés were the meeting points for the criminals to sell the proceeds of their crimes.

I couldn't believe my ears, and scribbled all this information frantically into my notebook.

'If you want any more information, come back,' said the father, as I left, head spinning.

Back at the station, I went straight to my inspector. Within twenty-four hours, he had transferred me to CID, the plain clothes unit. I was now an acting detective inspector.

The detectives of the Criminal Investigation Department consider themselves the aristocrats of the force. They call uniformed police 'woodentops', and have their own culture and their own rules which they protect fiercely. Luckily, I had something I could bring to CID that they needed: my information broke open an investigation into the local Asian gangs that was going nowhere.

One of the reasons that CID hadn't had much success investigating the Asian gangs up to that point was that it had few black and Asian officers. Part of the point of wearing plain clothes is to fit in with the community. None of them could have walked into a local café where my young informant told me I would find the ringleaders without attracting attention. So I was useful.

In fact, in my months in CID, the operation led to numerous arrests and the recovery of millions of pounds of stolen property. On one raid, we discovered four dismantled Porsches. We effectively put Superfly out of business, and he responded by letting anyone who would listen know that he would 'get Ali

Dizaei'. Eventually, we simply had to draw a line under the investigation, as it had snowballed to the extent that it threatened to overwhelm the resources that CID had for it.

CID was sometimes fun. I enjoyed the camaraderie immensely, joining in the jokes at the expense of the woodentops, while knowing that one day soon I would be a woodentop again. But if CID is the elite, their attitude to racist abuse was more shocking than the uniformed branch. CID in those days seemed to have an even bleaker vision of the outside world than the rest of the force. I vividly remember when I was custody sergeant trying to find a detective to deal with an Asian woman who was distraught because her young son had disappeared. Time after time I was told they were 'too busy'. When I threatened to tell the superintendent, the detective sergeant grudgingly agreed to come downstairs. He had his revenge though, shouting noisily, 'Where's the fucking Paki slag then?' as he walked down the stairs.

High Wycombe CID would daily express their disgust at the outside world, and the 'fucking niggers' and 'fucking Pakis' who inhabited it. When those conversations started, CID was not fun. In the last ten years, there has been a major change in the way the police force works: previously, 'tenure' decreed that if you were in a specialised branch, you were there for life unless you wanted to move. Today, that's no longer the case. By injecting fresh blood into units like CID, the worst excesses of the culture – which also bred laziness, insolence and even corruption – have been avoided, and the vast majority of detectives who are dedicated and fair can today work in a more positive environment.

While in the CID, I applied for the Accelerated Promotion Course. This would be my first step on to the fast track. Only a handful of officers from any force are selected to attend the APC, and I wanted to be in the class of 1992. I got my recommendation from Assistant Chief Constable George Hedges, who was not the first, nor the last, to praise me while noting that 'he should be kinder to people who are less intelligent than him', and 'he has a tendency to alienate himself because of his ability to argue a point'. When I went for the day of selection interviews, the group I was part of voted me as the most likely to be a future chief constable, but I got the least votes as someone they would want to go on holiday with.

APC was fifteen weeks at the Police College in Bramshill, followed by another ten weeks after you became an inspector. It was a revelation for me, everything I had hoped for: the course is all about law and management, not racist jokes and learning to march.

I was recommended for promotion in the shortest possible time: that would mean I could be an inspector in eighteen months. But instead, I wanted more experience, and volunteered for a year on the motorcycle wing of the traffic section; this was followed by my promotion, and taking on one of the first high-profile jobs that would make me enemies top-to-bottom in the force.

At Reading police station, Chief Superintendent Howell-Bolton, who was operational divisional commander, wanted me as his staff officer. In one way, it's a plum job. You control access to your boss, and it teaches you a lot about what command means. One of his initiatives was to find out which officers provoked the most complaints, and 'name and shame' them for everyone to see.

It was a great idea, but someone had to compile the information. That would be me. I had become accustomed to the occasional casual racism of the job, although it still hurt. I wasn't prepared for the outpouring of bile that I received in my mail when I took the job. Chief Supt Howell-Bolton praised me for my efforts. It seemed at the time that he was the only police officer in the whole of Reading who thought I was doing a good job. It was a relief to become a shift inspector again, and get back to day-to-day policing.

By February 1995, I thought I was ready for a new challenge as an inspector. I didn't know quite what I was taking on.

A gang is outside the police station, pelting it with stones and screaming race hate. Along Hart Street, Bell Street and New Street, shop windows have been shattered. The kids who broke the windows are doing some minor looting. In the centre of town, someone has thrown a brick through the window of a police car. There's fighting in the car park of the local pub and on the street corners.

We've responded with force: the police have their riot batons out. Police dogs are snarling at the ringleaders; we're making arrests.

It's 2 am on a Sunday morning in November 1995. But this isn't an inner-city ghetto or a football riot, it's the town centre of one of the wealthiest areas in the United Kingdom. On the whole, the kids who are arrested aren't deprived, or cursed by poverty or hopelessness. We're used to thinking that violent disorder, rioting and motiveless damage is done by an underclass with few opportunities and a lot of rage.

This damage was mostly done by a young, privileged elite. If anything, they were an overclass, living in the wealthy streets near the police station where I was an inspector, in Henley-on-Thames. Even the looting is different in Henley: one of the local shops had its window smashed and two teddy bears were taken.

For fifty-one weeks of the year, Henley minds its own business, a gentle, wealthy town west of London, home to wealthy retirees, stockbrokers and board directors. For many years, the ex-Beatle George Harrison lived a reclusive life in a large house on the edge of town. Many of the residents have lived in Henley for generations, relishing its old stone architecture and small-town comfort. For five days in July it briefly comes to the attention of the outside world, when the Henley Royal Regatta brings tens of thousands of revellers to the town on days out, wearing an informal uniform of straw boaters, old school blazers and caps matched with striped ties or brightly coloured cravats. They arrive in the morning, drink champagne and Pimms in marquees pitched by the river Thames, watch the world-class rowing events from deckchairs by the river bank, take afternoon tea at 4 pm, and pack into jolly, drink-sodden trains back into town, talking about how beautiful and untouched the old place is, how time has stood still in this corner of old England.

In September 1994, six months into my stint as a Thames Valley police inspector, I was dispatched to Henley sub-division to sort out problems that the day-trippers rarely saw, because Henley had a double life. By day, it was a town that had barely changed in 200 years. By night, posh binge drinkers were fighting on street corners, urinating in the gutter, running into the road in front of buses for fun, even assaulting the police in the market square. Many of the drinkers were taking drugs, bought in local pubs. Many of them were under age. At pub closing time at the weekend, the main streets of the town had become one of Britain's unlikeliest no-go zones for the public, a midnight freak show that proved that lager loutishness was not solely a problem of the working classes.

I decided that the softly-softly attitude which had previously tried to manage the problem wasn't working. It was getting worse, not better. A few weeks into the job in March 1994, I called all the local publicans together for a meeting.

'This cannot go on,' I told them. 'If you don't take note of who drinks in your pubs, we will have to take action.'

My officers had told me that a lot of the problem was the lax attitude that the pubs were taking to serving drinkers who were under age, serving them when they had already drunk too much, and not doing enough to cut out drug dealing in the bars. My message: we had to work together. I understood that it wasn't going to be easy for many of the landlords, but this was a serious situation, and the police couldn't solve it without their help. I was going to get that help, hopefully voluntarily, but if not, by any means necessary.

After our chat, the atmosphere in the town improved, thanks in great part to the licensees. Most were doing their best, and we backed this up with extra police on duty, and a police van parked in the town centre, ready to disgorge a group of coppers in seconds if there was any trouble. We weren't tyrants – it's a part of the British culture for youngsters to booze on a Saturday night, and we had to be tolerant of drunken behaviour as long as it didn't affect other people. In 1995, there was little flexibility in licensing hours, so at 11 pm, hundreds of loudly sozzled drinkers would all be thrown on to the street at the same time. When they were having a laugh, we stood by. When that laugh started to threaten other people, make them scared or uncomfortable, or threatened to turn into violence, we were going to arrest them, sending the message to the others that we're not tolerating this. Despite the long-standing problems, the landlords worked well with us. We were winning the battle in many of the local pubs.

There were still regular flashpoints. In June 1995, soon after the regatta crowds had moved on, the first 'Henley riot' kicked off. At that time, many of the UK's small towns were struggling to contain teenage drinking; and yet few places outside the big city centres, and nowhere with Henley's privilege and position, would witness violence to compare with November 1995.

The Three Tuns in Falaise Square would become the focus of our attempt to change the atmosphere in Henley. It was the most popular pub in town with young people, with a bar called 'The Stables' in which they liked to meet. Our informants were telling us that drug deals were commonplace there. It didn't help that the square outside the pub was the main point where drinkers congregated after closing time or that the licensee, Robin Gladman, who was a long-standing member of the community, didn't approve of our hard-line approach. Perhaps he didn't like being lectured by a 33-year-old upstart policeman – though for ten years, I had been a Henley resident too.

My relationship with the town's local politicians wasn't entirely smooth either. Soon after I arrived, I had declined an invitation to a sherry evening, reasoning that I was there to do a job, not to schmooze the mayor. Could I have taken a more conciliatory attitude? Possibly, but in my mind, this spirit of friendly cooperation was part of what had gone wrong in Henley, and my instructions were to bring a fresh approach. I argued for CCTV cameras in the town centre to record who was causing the trouble, or even better to discourage it in the first place, which the council, surprisingly, opposed. I began to wonder if their priorities were in the right order.

The disagreements continued. In the summer of 1995, Councillor Smewing, at that time the mayor, requested that cafés and restaurants in town should be stopped from putting tables and chairs outside so that tourists and locals could take advantage of the brief summer season. He argued that they caused an obstruction. I disagreed, and one result was that he obviously considered that *I* was causing an obstruction. Going over my head, he asked Sir Charles Pollard, the chief constable of Thames Valley (and a personal acquaintance of his) if there was any chance of removing 'this inspector' from his town. Sir Charles not only said that there wasn't, but wrote to his deputy, Ian Blair (now Sir Ian), who at that time was the assistant chief constable, to ask for his observations. ACC Blair supported my approach and wrote back to him, copying me in his letter. That boosted my confidence.

At least I knew that my enemies weren't just drunken loutish bottle-lobbers; but it seemed ironic that my hard-line stance, which on the surface appeared tailor-made for the traditional councillors of Henley-on-Thames, was meeting such a lot of opposition.

The final straw came when in March 1996, an undercover operation in the Three Tuns revealed widespread drug dealing was going on. We caught four men with cannabis and amphetamines in their wallets and underpants. A few months previously I had personally stopped two kids in the street outside the pub, both drunk. I asked them their age.

'Fifteen,' they told me.

The Three Tuns had its own ID scheme that allowed sixteen-year-olds who carried yellow cards into the Stables Bar as long as they didn't buy or drink alcohol. For eighteen-year-olds, there were ID cards that proved their age. The scheme obviously wasn't working.

On 19 August 1996, the local licensing magistrates in Thame revoked Gladman's licence after a week-long hearing, a decision which was later reversed on appeal.

Perhaps I was naive. I wasn't expecting a backlash. In my mind, I was doing the council and the residents of Henley a service. Maybe telling the press that the problem in town was caused by 'little Jeremys and little Henrys' in November 1995 had burnt my bridges with the mothers and fathers of some of those Jeremys and Henrys. Whatever the reason, the local councillors tried to have me fired.

Instead, the papers who covered the problem in Henley often chose to focus on the dispute between me and the council. For example, the *Guardian* on 27 September 1996 revealed that 'They are seeking a meeting with the Thames Valley chief constable to ask that Inspector Dizaei be transferred.'

The debate ran longest and keenest in the local newspaper, the *Henley Standard*. On 16 August, the same day as the licensing authorities were deciding on the future of the licence of the Three Tuns, the newspaper ran a series of interviews with people from the town who considered Gladman was hard done by. It alleged he had been 'made a scapegoat' and 'victimised by police'. One local resident accused me of having 'a vendetta' against the landlord.

On 6 September, Councillor Ken Arlett told the *Standard* that
'It's hardly a good advertisement for Henley. We have worked so
hard on tourism – yet this chap Inspector Dizaei seems to want
to destroy it. Another set of friends have asked me whether this
chap is on an ego trip. He obviously is.'

He accused me of being a 'crusader' – as if crusading for things
like an end to drunken brawling in the streets had suddenly
become a bad thing.

Councillor Arlett would not have been happy when TV crews
called to ask for my cooperation in news reports about the
problem, and I agreed. I even said yes to daytime chat shows. I
reasoned that pretending the problem didn't exist hadn't solved it,
so it was time to give it as much exposure as possible. Doing little
or nothing in the face of weekend rioting would not, in the long
run, encourage tourism, and meanwhile hundreds of innocent
people were being made miserable by the louts.

In the same article, the former Mayor Smewing told the
Standard that 'We have the wrong man for this town. He is the
right man for an inner-city area.' Not, it seems, one of us.

Meanwhile, our postbag was telling a different story to the
one that the councillors were telling the press, as local residents
congratulated us on our stance. When I walked down the street
of my home town, I would sometimes be stopped by locals who
would shake my hand. The same was true in the *Henley Standard*,
as readers wrote in to complain about their councillors: for two
weeks, the letters occupied two pages, with the majority being
in favour of our 'crusade', and critical of the councillors who
tried to stop it for the sake of the town's image with tourists.
One wrote to say he was 'stunned and disgusted'. Another was
'dismayed and angered'. Those four words would also sum up my
reaction to the councillors who tried to undermine our attempt
to civilise Saturday nights in what should have been one of the
most peaceful and beautiful towns in England.

5 Black and blue

It's 1997, and I'm driving my BMW through Southall, an area of West London with a large Asian community and a strong identity with it. It's a 30 mph limit, and I'm doing 35 mph on the way home from the gym. A police car flags me down.

'I'm sorry, officer,' I say, 'I was over the speed limit.'

'Can you step outside the car and tell me if you have any drugs on you, sir?' asks the officer who stops me.

I hadn't shaved that morning, but speeding while unshaven is not a legal basis to search my car for drugs, which is what the officer proposed to me as his next course of action. I told him that he wasn't allowed to do that. He swore at me, and the situation was getting heated as I reached for my warrant card, identifying me as an inspector in Thames Valley Police.

That changed the mood. 'I'm sorry, sir,' the officer says, 'you don't know what it is like out on the street. You can't be too careful.'

I did know exactly what it was like out there. I hadn't exactly had a sheltered life, and for nine out of my twelve years of service, I had been an operational police officer. I had spent my time on the street, just as these police officers had; it's just that I identified potential drug dealers using a different set of criteria.

The sour joke among the black and Asian population is that the police can stop you for the offence of 'driving while black'. Black police, black lawyers, black barristers, black businesspeople share a common experience of being pulled over by police officers and made to feel like a common criminal. I had been stopped like this three times in fourteen months; compared to the experience of some of my colleagues and friends, I'm pretty lucky that I haven't been stopped more often. My research among other police officers showed that half of us had been stopped or questioned by police officers while they were off duty; 13 per cent were not treated with respect by people who, at the time, did not know they were talking to a fellow officer. In their minds, the off-duty black officers they were addressing were suspects. If you are African or African-Caribbean, you are twenty-seven times more likely to be stopped by the police than if you are white. If you are Asian, you are eighteen times more likely to be stopped. The 'stop and search' powers which make it possible to stop youths in this way were created to deal with football hooligans and drug users at the 'raves' of the 1990s, but had since been used in a racially biased way. This is overall a tolerant, caring society; but the tolerant gloss can obscure a layer of deep-rooted racial prejudice that we'd rather not face.

It's the same for many other groups in the UK: how do we police the gay community? How do we treat women, both inside the force and in the community? These are questions that are uncomfortable to ask for many police officers, who claim that any bias is based on what it is like 'out on the street', not on pervasive and deeply ingrained prejudice.

If we don't face these questions, and try to answer them, then we build a long-term problem: the forces of law and order are recruited overwhelmingly from the white, male population; other groups often find very little in common with the values of that group. If what police officers consider to be 'normal' is different from what the communities they serve consider 'normal', then we all have a problem, because those communities won't think that police power is legitimate. Instead they see the police as an oppressive arm of the state, whose task is to discriminate against those who do not share their values. Inevitably respect for the law, and for the people whose job it is to enforce the law, declines.

The police rely entirely on intelligence and information to solve crime and bring criminals to justice. This is called community intelligence. If communities do not have trust in the police, they will not give the police the information we need, or agree to be witnesses, or attend identification parades. If we don't create a diverse, inclusive police force, we risk creating a society fractured along racial lines where hard-working, honest police officers can't do their job effectively. Without community intelligence we simply can't win the fight against crime.

It's August 1999, and I'm one of 2,000 black police officers marching through the streets of Toronto. Alongside me, my colleagues from the National Black Police Association. We're wearing the uniforms of the British police; alongside us, black officers who are proud to march in the uniforms of their local police forces from all over the United States and Canada. Even the Royal Canadian Mounted Police are represented, black Mounties on horseback.

As we walk through the deprived areas of Toronto, we're clapped and cheered. The black community lines the streets, encouraging us. We're moved, the emotion tightens our chests. For me, it was a feeling of belonging that I didn't always feel in London, the feeling of being part of a community that we wanted, but were often denied. When I was called 'Ayatollah' at Police College, when I received race hate mail in the internal post, having to face my colleagues in the knowledge that one or more of them was sending it, I was denied the feeling of belonging that most police officers take for granted.

I found that feeling on the streets of Toronto; more importantly, so did the black and Asian residents who cheered us. Our solidarity march helped legitimise policing in areas where it struggled for legitimacy; it created pride in what the black community is and what its members could aspire to be.

From the first day in the force, my colour and ethnic background had been a discussion point; it almost forced me to quit before I had become a probationer constable. Sometimes, in a force with few other black or Asian officers, I felt lonely, isolated and resentful. When other black officers began to organise into the National Network for black officers, the groups that would eventually coalesce to form the National Black Police Association, I was ready and willing; my activism had started a long time earlier, in 1990.

The success of the racial harassment surgery in Reading sparked my interest in race and recruitment to the police force. I thought this was an ideal topic to study for a master's degree – and if I did a good job, I could use what I learned in my work. I applied for a grant – called a 'Bramshill Fellowship' – from the police to study for an MA, but was refused. I didn't want to give up, so I started a master's degree in law and criminal justice in my own time. I asked for a grant to help with the cost – as a sergeant with a young family, I didn't have much money – but again, I was refused. I still have the letter. It says: 'the officer should concentrate on police work rather than academic studies'. Instead, I decided to combine the two. At the time, working nights in the custody suite, I could do both. When I wasn't on duty, I studied some more. It wasn't a great time at home for Natalie, as my work inevitably affected our relationship. It was when we realised we wanted different things from our lives, and that's when we separated.

After completing my master's degree in 1992, I had a taste for more research. I wanted to take the work I had done to a deeper level, researching whether there was racial discrimination in promotion and specialist jobs in the police force, how it occurred, and what could be done about the problem. Again, I had applied for a Bramshill Fellowship in 1994, and again I was denied it.

'Mr Dizaei,' said Assistant Chief Constable Dunn (who later became an assistant commissioner in the Met and a public supporter of Operation Helios), when I excitedly told him about the potential for my research, and how beneficial it could be, 'why do you have an obsession with race?'

Oh dear, I thought I had an obsession with fair and accountable policing. Again, I decided that I would complete my PhD in my own time, at my own expense.

The technique I used to collect research was simple, but it sapped your patience. Ethnographic anthropology is the jargon term, which effectively means going with the flow, immersing yourself, letting fellow officers talk freely, not challenging them; instead, when they talk to you honestly about their views, whether you agree or not, you can record them and use them to build an accurate picture of what your colleagues really think and feel. For any institution that has a potential problem with race, research like mine is a hard pill to swallow. Sometimes, I got all the access I needed. Other times, my work wasn't so easy: some senior officers stopped me from interviewing their staff, especially the black staff. Nevertheless, after three years of slog out of hours, I completed my thesis. Although having a PhD doesn't save you from getting stopped in Southall for driving while black, maybe it does gain you a little more respect.

In the meantime, the NBPA had been born. As far back as 1990, the Met Police had become alarmed at the numbers of black officers who were leaving the force. The black support network, with support from many of the senior officers in the force, first gave shape to the London Black Police Association in September 1994. 'I have made it clear where I stand,' said Sir Paul Condon, the commissioner of the Metropolitan Police, at the launch. At the time, being in Thames Valley, I couldn't be part of the London

BPA – but when the association started to hold meetings with officers from other forces a year later, my work on my PhD had got me interested. By October 1996, black officers had formed a national communication network, and adopted our motto, 'One voice, strength in unity'.

After a change of government, Jack Straw – at that time the home secretary – agreed to sanction and help fund the NBPA, and in November 1998 it finally became a reality. Our mission wasn't to create a divisive group within the force, although we knew many officers were suspicious of our motivation. We were, and still are, a professional organisation, similar to the ones that already existed: the Police Federation, which represents the lower and middle ranks; the Superintendents' Association; and the Association of Chief Police Officers, for the highest ranks. Our job wasn't to supersede those associations, or undermine them. We thought – and the home secretary agreed – that it was time our voice was heard alongside them. We would inevitably see policing and the experience of the community through a different lens, which we hoped would help the service to understand the reality of policing in multi-cultural Britain.

In truth, it was well overdue. Race had never been a more divisive problem inside the British police than following the murder of Stephen Lawrence in April 1993, and the subsequent investigation.

Stephen Lawrence was an A level student from Eltham in south-east London. In 1999 a public inquiry into the murder, chaired by former judge Sir William Macpherson of Cluny, described the crime in Chapter One of its findings:

'Stephen Lawrence had been with his friend Duwayne Brooks during the afternoon of 22 April. They were on their way home when they came at around 22:30 to the bus stop in Well Hall … Mr Brooks was part of the way between Dickson Road and the roundabout when he saw the group of five or six white youths who were responsible for Stephen's death on the opposite side of the road.

'Mr Brooks called out to ask if Stephen saw the bus coming. One of the youths must have heard something said, since he called out "what, what nigger?" With that the group came quickly across the road and literally engulfed Stephen. During this time one or more of the group stabbed Stephen twice.'

The killing was, in the findings of the inquiry, 'simply and solely and unequivocally motivated by racism. It was the deepest tragedy for his family. It was an affront to society, and especially to the local black community in Greenwich', and you would think it was an open-and-shut case. But investigating officers refused to accept that it was a hate crime, and in the course of a botched investigation left both Brooks and the Lawrence family feeling as if they were the criminals. Eventually, the gang of self-declared racists who most people assumed were responsible were charged with the murder – only for the case against them to be dropped because of a lack of direct evidence.

This investigation was, by any standard, a perfect example of poor leadership and incompetence. As the Macpherson report concluded, there was: 'a fundamental misjudgement and mistake made during the first three days after the murder in connection with the arrest of the suspects. Furthermore, the poor processing of the information which had come into the Incident Room during the first two days after the murder is plainly a matter for criticism.' The British public was also forced to confront the nasty fact that racist murderers not only existed, but could be protected by their community. This wasn't such a surprise for black members of the public, who perceived a police force that didn't take crimes against them seriously. Many people asked: how could this scandal happen?

The flaws in the investigation had threatened to undermine years of relationship-building between the police and the black community, but the Met resisted calls for a full public inquiry

until December 1997, when the Police Complaints Authority
issued a damning report into the investigation. That led to Lord
Macpherson's public inquiry, which met throughout the summer
of 1998. Sometimes an inquiry becomes a way to defuse tensions,
to create a 'safe' atmosphere in which the press loses interest in a
subject. In this inquiry, the opposite would be the case.

During the investigation I had made no secret of my view that
racism inside the police had been at fault. I had written many
times for the *Police Review* on the subject.

Although television cameras were not permitted at the inquiry,
the public interest in it was kept alive by press coverage, and a
nightly re-enactment of the drama on Channel 4. It helped that
the proceedings were a natural drama: when the accused gang
was called to testify in June, there were fights in the street, as
members of the Nation of Islam tried to enter the building. The
next day, they were pelted with bottles on their way into the
inquiry. The flamboyant performance of the Lawrence family's
barrister Michael Mansfield QC, a combative lawyer who
seemed to save his most withering performances for the cross-
examinations of the police officers who appeared before the
inquiry, heightened the public interest. The inquiry spent four
months investigating the investigation, calling sixty-five officers
– all of them white – to testify. Even at this stage, six refused to
accept any racial motivation in the murder, even though the
inquiry had seen secretly filmed footage of the gang playing with
knives and making abusive comments about black people.

The inquiry then spent as long investigating what lessons
there were for the British police. This boiled down to one simple
but unpleasant question: was the Metropolitan Police Service
institutionally racist? It was a question that was bound to split
the police force, and pitch officers against each other, in public.

In August 1998 Dr Robin Oakley, an advisor to the Met on race
who had also been my PhD examiner, testified that unintentional
and unspoken police racism had affected the investigation. But

while Sir Paul Condon had apologised to the Lawrence family for the first time in June, he still refused to concede this point.

John Newing, the chief constable of Derbyshire, and the chairman of a race relations task force that had been set up by ACPO, claimed in the *Observer* newspaper on 9 August that there was institutional racism, and that black people received an inferior service to white people. 'Unless smart people start understanding these issues, it's bound to affect how people approach problems…we pick on people because they appear to be different, and officers have a stereotype of them.'

At the NBPA, we were delighted: it was our opinion that the institutional racism was clear for anyone to see. Inspector Paul Wilson, the chair of the Metropolitan BPA at the time, called the statement 'refreshing'; 'I don't understand why the Met denies that institutional racism played a part in the Lawrence case,' he said.

The inquiry reached boiling point on 1 October 1998, when Sir Paul appeared before it: he 'deeply regretted' the failings of the investigation, he said, and he recognised the 'anger and frustration' of the black community.

'We have heard what people have been saying,' he said, 'and I accept that a central concern is that the Met is racist…I acknowledge that we have not done enough to combat racist crime and harassment.' But he didn't change the Met's position that the investigation into the murder was not compromised by institutional racism. If his apology was supposed to defuse the situation, and keep everyone happy, it had the opposite effect, as the parents of Stephen Lawrence reacted by calling for a new commissioner. 'We need someone to take radical action,' said Doreen Lawrence.

When the Macpherson report was published in February 1999 it contained some damning criticisms of the Met's attitude to racism: 'Upon all the facts we assert that the conclusion that racism played its part in this case is fully justified. Mere incompetence cannot of itself account for the whole catalogue of failure, mistakes, misjudgements, and lack of direction and control.'

And Lord Macpherson chose to criticise Sir Paul directly, saying his evidence 'placed too much emphasis upon individual racists and individual malpractice...there is a discernible difference between the approach of ACPO and other chief officers and the somewhat less positive approach of the commissioner.'

And he finished on a call to action for the government: 'We are confident that the home secretary and the government will perceive the pressures for change which this inquiry has uncovered, so the necessary transformations will start to take place.'

The contents of the report had been known for many months. All the Metropolitan Police could do was to brace itself for the criticism, convince the public that it was taking it seriously, and hope the story would go away. The report led the news for days, and the effect on the police force was devastating. Many officers, like Sir Paul, refused to accept that there were long-held attitudes in the police force that needed to change. If part of the problem in police culture was its tendency to bond together against a perceived attack from the black community, then the Macpherson report made this attack more real. It also gave a voice to the black community, both inside and outside the force.

Some commentators questioned whether the report should have been written, as the effect on the morale of police officers was a high price to pay. At the NBPA, we wondered where this concern for the morale of the police had been when many black officers, for years appalled by their treatment in the police force, had been giving up on their police careers and leaving the force.

I was, by that time, already devoting a large proportion of my time to being the vice-chairman of the NBPA. In the *Police Review* in January 1999, I had argued that many black police officers experience considerable suspicion and hostility when they stand up and discuss issues of discrimination and racism: 'It is not uncommon for their competence and motivation to be questioned when they genuinely and passionately believe things are not right. The NBPA could resolve some of these issues if police forces are willing to be pragmatic and cooperative.'

As part of my PhD research I had made contacts in the American BPA, and that had inspired me to keep pushing hard for change. We've been this way before, they told me, stick at it, this is how we succeed.

I was fully committed. I knew that if I was to join the Metropolitan Police, I would be in the middle of an organisation which was bruised and in some parts resentful of all the criticism it had received. I knew that by this time, I was the public face of much of that criticism, and didn't expect to be universally popular.

If I wanted to combine my role as an activist with my job as a senior police officer, my zeal disguised how naive I was. We were right, I thought, surely that's the most important thing. I was arrogant – I knew that there were people inside the Met who resented what I said, but I didn't think that resentment would be directed at me personally.

When I joined the Metropolitan Police Service, a service bruised from the Lawrence Inquiry but yet one that seemingly could not fully comprehend the steps that many of us thought it should take, perhaps it wasn't surprising that my own 'competence and motivation' would eventually be called into question.

Part three

Henley to Helios

1 **Too fat for the Met**

It wasn't only the councillors of Henley-on-Thames who thought I might be well suited to policing an inner city: but while they suggested it in an attempt to kick me out, I was delighted when London's top cop suggested it to get me in.

In 1998, I was back at Bramshill Police College. This time I wasn't studying, but on a temporary assignment, helping to teach the staff on the Accelerated Promotion Course. One of my jobs was to find guest speakers, and my best coup was to invite Sir Paul Condon, then commissioner at the Metropolitan Police, to give the constables and sergeants a talk. I was surprised when he agreed, and just as surprised when, over lunch, he asked me if I would consider transferring to the Met, because he thought I'd do well if I did.

I hadn't considered it before, but the Metropolitan Police Service offered me an outlet for my ambition, and perhaps it was the best place to try and use some of the ideas that I was having about how police work could be done. I had been approved for promotion to superintendent, but was frustrated, waiting for an opportunity in Thames Valley, where I had been happy – but where some of what I thought was my most important work had been politely sidelined. So in November 1998, when I saw that the Met was advertising for superintendents, I applied.

Superintendent Paul Toland called me two weeks later.

'We can't consider your application,' he told me.

I was too fat, he explained. At 6 ft 1 in tall and 243 pounds, the charts in his office showed that I must be carrying a lot of body fat. A standard body-mass index chart would define me as 'obese', but I was in great shape. I trained at my local gym almost every night. Perhaps it was my trip over from Iran with the weightlifting team, but I was an obsessive weight trainer. I lived a pretty dull life by many standards. I didn't drink or smoke, and kept my social life to weekends, but I loved to train. I had only 8 per cent body fat. I told Supt Toland about my body fat, but he wasn't impressed.

'If you want to be considered in the future, lose three stone,' he said.

I went to my doctor and had a medical, and showed the results to Supt Toland, who still thought – having consulted the Metropolitan Police policy – I was too fat, even though the notes from my doctor said I was in great shape. I told him that I was still going to turn up for my assessment.

At which point, my application was refused a second time. I had been downgraded from 'exceptional' to 'ordinary' on the basis of my communication skills. This looked like a joke: the evidence I had submitted included my master's and PhD commendations, my speeches, sometimes by this time sharing the podium with government ministers, and 100 TV and radio interviews. In Thames Valley, this was considered exceptional. In the big city, my communication skills weren't even considered acceptable.

Eventually, I argued my way to the assessment centre, where I took the day-long test, which centred on a practical exercise. I was delighted: the exercise involved my playing the role of a superintendent handling a suspected race crime.

I had, at the time, literally written the book on handling race crime in the British police, having just finished drafting a manual on it for the Association of Chief Police Officers; so it's fair to say that the exercise was something I was familiar with. After an interview with Commander Hugh Orde (now Sir Hugh, the chief constable of the Police Service of Northern Ireland) I went back to Thames Valley and waited, excited, for my pass.

Two weeks later, I got a letter to tell me that I'd failed the exercise.

I could have slunk off back to Thames Valley. Whoever failed me would have preferred that. But that wouldn't really be like me. So instead, I wrote to Sir Paul Condon to point out that I was having trouble fulfilling his wish that I should join, and that I couldn't understand why I was failing. He suggested I go to see Deputy Assistant Commissioner Barbara Wilding (now the chief constable of South Wales Police), the head of personnel, so that the Met could learn from my experience.

DAC Wilding took the trouble to write to me in advance to warn me not to complain to her in the language I used with Sir Paul, which, when I saw her, I ignored. 'Put this behind you and move on,' she suggested.

I suggested firmly in return that I wouldn't do any such thing, which didn't get a positive response.

'You'd better get out of my office right now,' she suggested, rather more forcefully. I took the hint, and left.

One week later, I was speaking at a conference, when I bumped into Commander Orde. 'Can you believe this man didn't get through his assessment?' he joked to my colleagues, adding, 'The decision wasn't down to me, I assure you.'

A few moments later, I'm standing in front of Sir Paul. 'How did the meeting with DAC Wilding go?' he asked.

'Did you send me there to be humiliated?' I said, attempting to disguise my irritation with the man I wanted to be my boss, and failing. This wasn't exactly the answer he was expecting, and when I explained, he fixed an appointment for me to come and see him to discuss it. Hopefully this time I would leave New Scotland Yard without being told to 'get out'.

I was frustrated because my career in Thames Valley seemed

to have stalled. I had good experience, great references and had passed every course and exam that I had studied for. But gradually, it became apparent that the praise and the letters of commendation I had received didn't translate into the responsibility I craved.

I had been picked, while still at Henley, to write a paper on what the culture of the police force should be. My paper concluded with the idea that a senior officer should take the research further. My chief constable, Sir Charles Pollard, liked the paper, and liked the idea, and told his personnel department to find a chief inspector to do the job.

So: I had done the initial research. I was waiting for a chief inspector's job. I had recently completed an MA in the subject, and was halfway through researching my PhD. Surely I was the man for the job.

Apparently not. The feedback I received was that Thames Valley Police didn't want to 'ghettoise' the subject by giving it to a black or Asian officer. I was crushed: as other inspectors received their promotions before me, my over-confidence got a severe correction. For a year and a half, I waited to become a chief inspector, with no joy. I eventually got my promotion in January 1997.

In December, I got a new posting that I thought would be perfect for my skills. I was to research new ways to run policing in the force: to concentrate on solving problems before they lead to crimes, rather than spending all our time trying to solve crimes that had already been committed. It's a good idea, but it requires a huge change in the culture of the police force. Officers would have to cooperate with other agencies, some of which – for example the social services – would traditionally be treated with suspicion.

Problem-solving policing can be simple: if there is a car park where cars are broken into, then ask the operator of the car park to install better lighting. When domestic disputes occur, try to make sure that someone is given the job of helping the couple sort out their differences, rather than break up the fight and wait to be called out again, maybe this time for a serious assault. It is about dealing with causes rather than symptoms.

I thought the idea could be used inside the force too, to make it real to every PC in Thames Valley. An example would be to cut the number of employment tribunals that happen because officers think they are overlooked for promotion. Too many officers become disenchanted when they feel they are unfairly overlooked, but it's nobody's problem, and the resentment eventually translates into a tribunal case which destroys any trust between the officer and his employers. My advice was that if there was a procedure to manage the problem, then fewer talented police officers would leave, and mistakes would be spotted and corrected.

My research showed that the biggest problems were in CID and the firearms units, where there was an 'old boy network' which had undermined some promising careers because a good officer's face didn't fit. I thought this was wrong, that it was a good place to start problem-solving, and when I presented my idea to the chief superintendents, I thought they would agree wholeheartedly. They hated it. Perhaps I should have seen it coming – after all, they were products of the system I was criticising.

Then I really did it, by doing research into the finance department, and discovering that every expense claim was checked seventeen times, no matter how petty it was. It seemed a strange way to treat officers who made life-or-death decisions every day. My conclusion was that police officers were treated like idiots at best, and at worst like potential fraudsters, every time they claimed for a meal. If I had tried to pick a topic designed to wind up my superiors more effectively, with hindsight I don't think I could have chosen better.

That's partly why, having passed my superintendent's selection process and having been recommended for promotion, I thought a fresh start in the Met might be a good idea.

In January 1999, I sat in Sir Paul's eighth-floor office, feeling suitably intimidated. It smelt old, like a library, decorated with wood panels. Outside, three secretaries plus a private secretary, an armed protection officer and a staff officer who outranked me took care of the commissioner's everyday needs. Inside: me, my anger having been replaced by the appropriate degree of intimidation, and Dave McFarland, the national coordinator of the NBPA, who I had brought as a witness. By this time, I was beginning to worry about the motives of whoever had failed me, and I was routinely keeping logs of my conversations, time and date stamped.

And the meeting did decide the rest of my career, but not in the way I had expected.

I put my case to Sir Paul. I showed him my qualifications, and told him what had happened. I was going over the head of the people who failed me, pushing and pushing because that's the only way I knew how to react. My pride wouldn't let me give up, because the more I thought about it, the more I thought I was right.

Sir Paul agreed. He leaned back in his chair and slapped his head. 'This is madness,' he said, and promised to call my chief constable in Thames Valley.

If I came to the Met, I asked, would I be victimised?

'If you do join the Met, I'll personally make sure that no one bothers you,' he said. 'I'll see you on a monthly basis.'

As we left, Dave McFarland said, 'I reckon you'll get in the Met, but you've made a lot of enemies.'

I was so naive that I had no idea what he meant. 'There are a lot of people going to be in deep shit over this,' he said. 'Condon isn't going to let this go.'

It was, to be fair, a tricky political problem for Sir Paul. He was about to be savaged by the Macpherson report. I was the leading spokesperson for the NBPA on the culture of racism in the police. I had just had my application to join the Met refused in circumstances that looked to me very much as if I was being singled out for special treatment from one or more of his staff. Whoever got the first phone call from Sir Paul after I left the office probably wouldn't thank me.

Shortly afterwards, I was invited to speak to twenty-five chief constables in a meeting held at Windsor Castle. The home secretary was there, the chief inspector of constabulary, the permanent secretary at the Home Office, and a gaggle of civil servants. The idea was to look at the criteria by which chief constables were appointed. My speech was about how they should be aware of race problems: as I pointed out, 75 per cent of white Britons preferred not to live next door to a black person, and 50 per cent agreed with voluntary repatriation. It was a heady experience. I wasn't even a superintendent yet, and I was being asked to sit on the working group on how chief constables were appointed.

At 7.30 pm, my mobile rang.

'Please hold, Mr Dizaei, the commissioner would like to speak to you.'

Sir Paul came on the line.

'I've reviewed your case,' he said. 'I'm offering you a job. Delighted to have you on board.'

The next day, I spoke to Patricia Woods, the director of human resources at the Met. She was attending the same conference. It was one month before the report of the Macpherson inquiry was due out. We all knew that Sir Paul was going to come under fire. The rumour – not true – was that the NBPA would call for his resignation.

Ms Woods suggested we find a quiet corner to speak. After congratulating me on my appointment she asked me, casually, if

I would be calling for Sir Paul's resignation. It would, she pointed out, be helpful to know – now I was one of them.

I tried to point out that I wasn't 'one of them' yet, and even if I was, I couldn't talk to her about NBPA business. The conversation did not go well. It was the first indication that my two jobs in the Metropolitan Police Service – as a superintendent and as a Black Police Association activist – were, in the eyes of many of my bosses, no longer compatible.

I might have been naive, I might simply have failed to see how much I was distrusted among my colleagues, and I was certainly unprepared for how that lack of trust was going to manifest itself; but at least I was no longer too fat for the Met.

2 The wrong tiepin

I joined the Met on 29 March 1999. Superintendent Toland was in charge of getting me a uniform and a warrant card, and showing me round. When I met him, he icily pointed out that my complaint about his behaviour had been read out in front of the Management Board chaired by the commissioner, which must have been a serious embarrassment for him.

A few weeks later, I was on the fast track again, thanks to Sir Paul Condon.

I was at my monthly meeting with Sir Paul which, true to his word, he kept. On 23 April, he surprised me by telling me he was 'proud of me', and offered a suggestion: why didn't I apply for the rank of commander? 'I believe you've got the ability,' he said.

This was, by any measure, ridiculous. I had been a superintendent for six weeks and a Met officer for less than four. Applying to be a commander would mean completing a command course, and being selected for that course, and would mean skipping a rank. It meant going through a process known as 'Extended Interviews' – a ten-day course by which you are assessed for your suitability to be trained as a senior police officer. I would be on the course with officers who had twice the length of service I did, and who had probably been superintendents for almost as long as I had been in the force. Was I being given the chance as a token black? It was possible. It was also very likely I would fail EI, in fact this was the most likely outcome. Sir Paul himself hadn't passed first time.

If I thought it was odd, there were many others in the Met who not surprisingly didn't care for my sudden elevation as Sir Paul's project. I might have only been in the Met a month, but I knew some people resented me, most of whom I hadn't met yet. I had no idea how keenly they felt that resentment. I had already made enough enemies to last a whole career.

One of the senior officers at Thames Valley had once warned me about my habit of speaking out. 'One of these days,' he said, 'someone will do your knees in.' Was this a friendly warning? It didn't sound like it. When I arrived at the Met, I arrived with two roles: one as the ambitious copper who wants to succeed in the force; the other as the spokesman for the NBPA with a remit to criticise the shortcomings in the police attitude to race when we saw it. The Met, by common consent, had a lot of shortcomings.

Inevitably I would be working alongside white officers who felt persecuted. Some had been singled out for special criticism by the press who were following the inquiry into the Stephen Lawrence murder investigation, including the man I was working for, Assistant Commissioner Ian Johnston, who was deluged with press attention as the officer responsible for handling the response to the inquiry findings. Under hard questioning by Michael Mansfield QC, who was acting for the Lawrence family during the inquiry hearings, his carefully measured tone had slipped and he had seemed to confirm the prejudice of police officers in London: districts with high crime in London, he said, were often populated by coloured people.

When he heard I was joining the Met, he had suggested I become his staff officer – in effect, his 'eyes and ears' in the force. His secretary Christine wasn't a fan of my NBPA work, I soon found out. She wasted no time in telling me that I wasn't to use the phone or fax machine for NBPA business, as she later admitted under cross-examination.

Race was beginning to define me in the eyes of many more senior officers too. On the one hand, I was proud of this. I wanted to make a difference, and I sincerely believed that this was a moment at which the police had to change, and I could influence that change.

Maybe, privately, many of the senior police officers who I thought I was helping considered me an upstart, a troublemaker. After the Lawrence Inquiry, the press was full of news of a crisis of morale in the police force, with critics suggesting that if the police admitted to failures in race relations it would cause more damage than if they didn't, because the black and Asian communities would lose confidence in the police force. For anyone who believed that point of view, I was a traitor to the force, a sixth columnist undermining it from within.

At least I wasn't hiding. One week before my meeting with Sir Paul I had attended the conference that was the culmination of four months of work I had done in writing the targets for recruitment and retention of black and Asian officers, so that by 2009 every force would have the number of officers that represented the racial make-up of the community in which it worked. The chief constables of those forces would be assessed based on their performance in meeting those targets, and could lose their jobs if they didn't meet them. Gloucestershire needed five more black or Asian officers, Durham six and Suffolk none at all.

The Metropolitan Police needed 5,662 more.

Jack Straw, the home secretary, presented the targets at a press conference, admitting that they were a 'challenge', but telling the assembled chief officers that the targets simply had to be met. I was given twenty minutes to speak immediately after him. 'Less than 1 per cent of you have read a black or Asian newspaper,' I told them, 'less than 3 per cent of you know or socialise with a black or Asian person, so please don't be upset when these communities don't openly trust you to decide what is right for them.' Jack Straw wrote me a note of congratulation, which I kept. In the evening, I was invited to a drinks party which excluded many of the chief constables I had spoken to earlier. I was excited for myself, but I don't think many of them shared my excitement, because at breakfast the next morning the five chief constables on my table didn't even say 'good morning' to me.

Nine out of ten officers on EI are chief superintendents. I would be by far the most junior officer on it, if my application was successful. AC Johnston clearly thought I wasn't ready when I hurried to his office to tell him the good news. He had been incredibly welcoming, going out of his way to provide me with an office, transfer unused leave days and let me use his car and driver when I needed it. This, though, was too much.

'Well, if the commissioner says you have to go, you have to go,' he said, eyebrows raised. I went to write my application.

At the same time, I received an unexpected request: Chief Superintendent Stephen Otter (now the deputy chief constable of Avon and Somerset) wanted me to come and work with him in Kensington and Chelsea. I had known him since we were part of the class of 1992 at the Accelerated Promotion Course. He'd been promoted faster than me, and he was in charge of three police stations in one of the wealthiest and most important areas of London. Kensington and Chelsea has many important residents, including the Queen. Harrods is in it, as are most of London's embassies.

The area was also familiar to me because that's where many of London's expatriate Iranians live. There are 30,000 Farsi speakers in the area, together with the Iranian Embassy, Iranian banks and around thirty Iranian restaurants. It was in one of those restaurants – owned by my uncle – that I met Chief Supt Otter in May 1999 for a meal to discuss how we would work together. 'You can't be serious,' he said when I told him I was applying for EI. He hadn't applied yet, and he was my boss. It must have been uncomfortable for him.

I was serious, I said, and my job in Kensington wasn't going to be straightforward either. I told him that as I was applying for EI, I was going to apply for promotion to chief superintendent as soon as possible. I was also not the most useful number two, as 50 per cent of my time was officially being spent on NBPA service for the immediate future. He'd have to accept, I said uncomfortably, that I wouldn't be around a lot of the time.

Thirdly, I was going to be dropped into the middle of my community, a group of people who I had been socialising with all my life. Often I went to my uncle's restaurants. My gym was in Kensington, and I sometimes went to a club called Tramp that was nearby. I was unusual among expats, who tended to become doctors or lawyers if they wanted to succeed: it wasn't just my father who thought the life of a police officer was no way for an ambitious Iranian boy to prove himself. If my fellow Iranians found me unusual, they were also proud of my progress, and I was invited to parties and gatherings at local businesses. The culture is very different to British culture: many members of the community claimed to know me or my father, or be related to me; people would stop me in the street and shake my hand; if I ate in a restaurant run by a member of my family, it would be impossible for me to pay without insulting them. Iranians can be extremely generous, and people would send me simple gifts, like a cake. I wasn't going to give anyone in the Iranian community special consideration, but it might not seem that way to anyone looking in from the outside.

Chief Supt Otter said he wanted me anyway.

My list of objections got down to the final item: where would I park my car? I lived in Henley-on-Thames, and unless I drove, the commute to work could take hours. The police station had space for three cars, and local car parks were ruinously expensive.

'That doesn't matter,' he said, 'I'll give you permission to park in the yard.' Sometimes the most innocuous decisions can have unforeseen consequences; but in the meantime, I transferred out of my plush staff officer's office with its view of the river Thames, and into Kensington police station. If I thought this was going to be equally plush, I was very much mistaken. And if I thought that Chief Supt Otter's generosity in accommodating all my wishes showed how much I was welcome in Kensington, the excitement of applying for EI was affecting my judgement.

I had only been in the job a few weeks when the problems around my NBPA involvement started to surface. Chief Supt Otter wasn't happy when I was absent in Chicago, attending a conference, and lots of officers took exception when I used the opportunity to suggest that the NBPA should work to educate young black people about their rights when they are stopped and searched by police officers. I was already getting hate mail at the station from officers who resented my car being parked in the crowded yard, while other officers took the tube.

Those officers also felt under constant pressure. One of the press reactions to the Stephen Lawrence Inquiry was that the Met wasn't just institutionally racist, it was institutionally incompetent as well. It wasn't unexpected – though depressing – that police officers, good and bad, would close ranks. When they did, I was on the outside, as were the other representatives of the NBPA.

As the year dragged on, I was involved in constant petty arguments with my boss. I drank my tea from a BPA mug, which Chief Supt Otter disliked. He also objected to my BPA tiepin. Police officers like to have their own tiepins: in uniform, it's a way to show a little character. Some wear Police Federation pins, some wear Rupert Bear tiepins. Traffic officers have their own special 'Black Rat' tiepin. Otter didn't think I should wear my BPA tiepin, though I wasn't wearing it as a challenge. I was wearing it because I was proud of the good work we were doing.

Our cordial Iranian meal seemed a distant memory when Chief Supt Otter called me to his office one day and told me that I could no longer park my car in the station yard. He had had too many complaints, he said. From now on, I would have a resident's parking permit, and would have to park my car anywhere I could find a space, often more than half a mile away. I couldn't understand why our relationship was turning so sour, so quickly. Yet Chief Supt Otter, as my supervisory officer, gave me a glowing review on my EI application. AC Johnston pushed it through with the lowest grade possible. I was going on EI.

3 Ethnic cleansing

Extended Interviews were held at Eastbourne. It's a four-day course, quite unlike anything you have experienced as a police officer before. You're not graded on your experience; you're graded on your potential to command.

You're also not graded exclusively by your fellow officers; you're assessed by a group of lay advisors as well. It seemed that everything I did created conflict in my two roles: I was about to attend the course, but I had also been given the job by the Home Office – which, with the ACPO, runs the course – of assessing the methods used to grade the people on it. When I saw how the future leaders of the British police were scored, I couldn't believe my eyes.

The process was unscientific and simplistic, and obviously hadn't been updated in years. Candidates were asked questions such as what the phrase 'Watch out, there's a Humphrey about' referred to. Confused, I looked it up to find that it was used in advertisements for Unigate milk that had last been aired in the mid 1970s. An army of red and white straws would sneak up and steal your milk. British officers of a certain age, who had watched television when they were young, might remember. Officers who weren't born in the country, or were younger, would have no idea. How this showed your suitability to become one of the country's most senior police officers was a mystery. The assessors were overwhelmingly white, Christian males aged fifty and above, and the exercises were set up so that you scored well if you happened to share their norms and values as well as meeting their expectations.

The non-service assessors, I discovered, were retired military men and high-ranking civil servants, who had been appointed by invitation, rather than having to be assessed themselves to show they had the ability to do a good job. They had undoubtedly been talented in their field, but that didn't mean they were the best people to choose the future leaders of the police force in a society which was changing rapidly, and would continue to change. They certainly did not have much in common with me. Meanwhile, the process had become fossilised. It had not been audited to make sure it did not unwittingly discriminate against people from different racial backgrounds. My report criticised the process; I was now going on the course and attacking it at the same time. I gave an interview to the *Police Review* on the subject, and the late Sir John Hoddinott, then the chief constable of Hampshire and the person in charge of the course, raged about it in an angry meeting with me at the Home Office. I might never have got close to passing EI, but a new regime was taking over, and Sir John's successor admitted that I had a point. Meanwhile, I had my own career to look after.

The Grand Hotel in Eastbourne, like the EI process, was a stately hangover from a bygone era. So it was entirely appropriate that the assessors lodged there. The candidates, myself included, stayed downtown. I was lonely and apprehensive. No one from my APC course in 1992 was on the EI, and no officers from the Met with whom I had a working relationship. They knew each other well, I didn't really know anyone. I was confident that I had done my preparation well – I had taken leave for a month to study – but I was tripped up by a question asking who Bart Simpson's mother was. I didn't watch *The Simpsons*, and I couldn't understand why this was any more relevant than knowing what a Humphrey was. In other ways, the exercises suited my experience: one involved writing a report under time pressure – our exercise was to write a report recommending which site of three a hospital should be built on. The trick isn't to try and use all the information, but to pick the most relevant facts quickly. I was also asked to role-play the chairman of a PR firm, advising a minister. But the funniest part of the process for me was my interview with a non-service advisor. I was given a titled retired army general. It wasn't a meeting of minds.

'What do you do for a hobby?' he asked me.

'Body building,' I said, 'and I like to write articles for magazines and newspapers.'

He searched his mind for a follow-up question on either topic; and finding none, moved on.

'Do you visit art galleries,' he asked, 'or any National Trust properties with friends and family on a Sunday afternoon?'

Now it was my turn to be struck dumb. Were the police looking to promote art experts?

'Sir, the idea is about as alien to me as pumping iron is to you,' I told him, as politely as possible.

While I thought I had done well at EI, it confirmed my suspicion that the assessment procedures were those of a society that no longer existed. I was on a mission, and I didn't stop to think about the consequences of the problems I was raising, or to worry about the result of what was becoming a nasty conflict of interest. That was going to reach a crescendo with the reaction to a speech that was to become a millstone around my neck, when I accused the police of 'ethnic cleansing'.

It's 29 November 1999. I'm on stage at the Birmingham International Convention Centre giving a speech in front of 2,000 black officers, the home secretary, hundreds of civilian colleagues and many senior police officers, including Chief Supt Otter, at the first NBPA conference. I have been vice-chairman for a year, and have just been confirmed as the association's legal advisor. Neville Lawrence had earlier received a standing ovation when he called on the police to win back the reputation it had when he arrived in Britain in the 1960s, when he wouldn't have thought twice about asking a police officer for help. 'That doesn't happen today,' he said.

The conference wasn't about destroying the police force, it was about wanting to make it better. We were all police officers. In our minds, we were on the inside, working to improve the situation by articulating the hard truths that stared us in the face – although to some it looked as if we were doing our best to destroy the police force they knew. The truth was, as I was about to say in my speech, that the police force they knew was destroying our careers. As black staff we were not the problem but part of the solution.

During 1999, the NBPA had accepted in many interviews that efforts were being made to solve the problems highlighted by the Stephen Lawrence Inquiry. One of the toughest problems to solve, and one which I had been researching now for more than five years, was what happened to bright black and Asian police officers who wanted promotion. In 1998, sixty-eight police officers had gone to a tribunal to accuse their employers of racial discrimination. In the previous four years, not one black officer had gone through the accelerated promotion scheme, and out of 102 applicants from the black and Asian community, only two had received interviews. My research showed a clear cultural bias in the selection procedures used. I could talk with authority: not only had I researched it, but I had lived through the experience. Black and Asian officers took longer to get promoted, and minor problems, which for a white officer would often be handled with a quiet word or an informal chat, would too often escalate into senseless disciplinary procedures that left a stain on their record and mutual animosity.

It wasn't about preferential treatment for blacks and Asians, it was about a waste of talent, about fairness at work.

It was also not a one-man crusade or an ego trip for me. I believed, and still believe, that our community, black and white, young and old, able or disabled, deserves a police service with competent leaders – not least because those leaders are not elected, and yet every day they take decisions which affect all our lives.

'There is not one black officer on the fast-track scheme, and the people who join the fast-track system today will become the senior officers of tomorrow,' I said, adding that there was a chickenwire mesh at the top of the service. The officers in my audience could see success, but they couldn't reach it. I told them about the Humphrey, and Marge Simpson (who I had subsequently found out was Bart's mother). I accused the police of 'ethnic cleansing' – ensuring that there was no way through to the highest ranks of the force for most black and Asian officers.

Afterwards, I received a commendation from the home secretary. When the newspapers reported my comments the next morning, many of my colleagues at Kensington were less excited. They let me know how they felt, in abusive terms, through the internal mail in the police station. Some of them were also letting Chief Supt Otter know that they didn't like working with a police officer who held those views. On 2 December 1999, he called me to his office. He had been 'inundated' with complaints after my speech, he said. I told him that I wasn't speaking at the conference as his number two in the police station, but as part of my role in the NBPA. It was every bit as much my job to do that. I had, I pointed out, received a standing ovation at the time, so some of my colleagues had liked what I had to say. He knew, because he was there. Were the complaints, I asked, from white officers?

The content of the newspaper reports was turning sour in some cases too. The veteran ex-minister Norman Tebbit, famous for suggesting we should test the patriotism of non-whites in the UK by asking them which national cricket team they would support, wrote an article asking if the selection process for senior officers in Iran was better than the one I was criticising.

While I wasn't getting support from senior officers over my speech – with hindsight, they were probably as angry, if a lot more subtle, as the idiots who pinned newspaper articles to my door – I wasn't getting any official complaints. That is, unless you count the complaint of Chief Constable Dame Elizabeth Neville, who was now in charge of EI. In December 1999, AC Johnston called me to his office. He had received an official complaint, he said, from CC Neville about my speech. In mentioning the question about Bart Simpson, I had given away one of the confidential answers. She was not happy. AC Johnston felt embarrassed raising it and I did not want to add to his embarrassment, so I kept a straight face while being gently admonished for this breach of confidentiality.

It was a relief during this time to get out of the police station, but many of the other activities I was involved in weren't going to ease the tension back at base. On 8 December, I received one of the most exciting invitations of all: I was invited to 10 Downing Street to meet the prime minister and his wife, to attend a seminar on what it meant to be 'British'. Afterwards, a newspaper article about the occasion which mentioned my name was pinned to my door. 'Fucking tosser' was scribbled across it. Whoever did it wasn't referring to Tony Blair.

Three days previously, I had received the letter which seemed to make all this aggravation, argument and conflict worthwhile. I had passed EI, first time. I was the first superintendent with less than a year's service to pass. I was elated. There was a caveat: before I attended the Senior Command Course, which would prepare me for a commander's job, I would have to do another year of service to get more experience in command at an operational level. So I would spend a year in charge of a borough with 'total operational command', and then enter the SCC in April 2001, the board suggested.

In January 2000, I was given this feedback personally by a senior civil servant, who told me that my new role must be one in which 'the buck stops' with me. I was making notes, because I was sure there was something amiss. Back at Kensington, the sour atmosphere wasn't the only odd behaviour I saw. Sergeant Kibblewhite, someone who I considered a troublemaker and a gossip, was Chief Supt Otter's staff officer; and my secretary – who was in on the gossip that I was excluded from – warned me that he was making trouble for me, chatting with the other officers about how I was getting preferential treatment, and cutting articles from the newspapers to show them. Chief Supt Otter seemed to notice a lot more things about me that he didn't like. My belt wasn't regulation issue (I hadn't been issued with one when I joined). I rolled my sleeves up at work. I received too many calls from the public. I wondered how he had the time to see all these things, and wondered how much negative information Sgt Kibblewhite was passing on.

If a deferred pass couldn't satisfy my desire to climb the ladder as quickly as I wanted, it offered one wonderful opportunity: the chance to get away from Kensington police station and the poisonous atmosphere that surrounded me.

In this situation, I met with my bosses to request my new posting. I made no secret of the fact that I wasn't happy at Kensington, but I now had two letters from the EI panel to say that I should be given command of a borough. No good, they said, it wasn't fair on a borough to have someone run it for a year before going somewhere else. Later, I was told by them that the EI recommendation had changed, and it wouldn't be necessary to run a borough after all. AC Johnston said he had 'something else in mind' for me. This sounded ominous.

On 8 February 2000, I found out what it was. The Met

had called a special meeting to decide my 'development plan', where they told me that the 'something else' was to become a superintendent in charge of operations – at Kensington police station. I met with Chief Supt Otter the next day to tell him that I wanted to apply for chief superintendent vacancies, which I was entitled to do, and he warned me that the Met wouldn't be keen: after all, I had just committed myself to a new job in my current location. There was to be a special assessment for me every ten weeks. Superintendents are assessed normally once a year: I was to be assessed twice, when to the best of my knowledge I didn't need this extra assessment, and no one could give me a reason why I did.

I felt as if someone was watching me. I hadn't done anything wrong that anyone had told me about, but I was very obviously becoming a 'problem'. I had made speeches and represented black officers in tribunals, but that was my job. If I was outspoken, I was speaking the same language as many prominent politicians. The NBPA position on the campaigns I was involved with was usually consistent with the policy of the police force, if not with its day-to-day reality. If that reality didn't live up to the ideals of the police force – and I said so because that was my job – I figured that was their problem, not mine.

Perhaps I figured wrong. All I knew was that I wasn't being permitted to leave Kensington.

When the Met advertised for chief superintendents – and I was already in the Met, qualified and keen – I applied. It made sense. If I was ready to be a commander, then passing the chief superintendent promotion process – one step below – should logically have been simple. It was 17 February 2000. Five days later, Chief Supt Otter, who was leading the selection panel, told me that he wouldn't support my application for a chief superintendent role, and that I wasn't being put forward – although I didn't get an official letter to tell me the truth until 6 April, when I had no choice but to take up the job in Kensington if I didn't want

to jeopardise my chances of getting on to the command course
twelve months later.

When I saw the assessment form, I couldn't believe my eyes.
When I compared it to my EI application, it was almost identical
in the questions it asked, and so I simply cut-and-pasted my
experience and suitability from one form to the other. Chief Supt
Otter had added his comments. On the EI form, he had given me
a glowing reference. A few months later, his comments made me
out to be a fantasist ('this had led him to occasionally exaggerate
his contribution to the events cited') and warned that I was
refusing to cut back on my NBPA role.

I thought he had sabotaged me, but I could not understand
why – not least because Chief Supt Otter, who was ambitious,
would not want to be vulnerable to a claim of discrimination if
I went to an employment tribunal. And of all people, he knew
that I would go that far. There must have been something that
allowed him to feel secure when he took that risk.

And surely he would be pleased to be rid of me, I thought.
If he believed these things, why had he not put them on paper
when I was applying for EI? I avoided him, and we barely spoke.
I stopped telling him when I was going to be out of the office on
NBPA business, which I had previously done as a courtesy. The
time for courtesy had passed.

I showed the two forms to my mentor in the force, an assistant
commissioner I had known for many years called Tariq Ghaffur.
AC Ghaffur and I had completely different attitudes to this type
of problem. He didn't seek conflict, but picked his battles very
carefully; I respected his attitude, but when – I reasoned – there
were so many important battles to fight, I found it impossible to
be as accommodating as AC Ghaffur was. Nevertheless, he was a
good influence on me, several times counselling caution when I
was impetuous.

Seeing the two forms spread out in front of him in his office
in Kingston, even AC Ghaffur was concerned to see two sets of

irreconcilable opinions written by the same officer inside a few months. He wrote a note, which I kept.

'Smells of a personal vendetta,' it said.

One week later, I had another meeting with the top brass, where I asked for an outside assessor to look at the way I was being held back. Afterwards I called AC Ghaffur; I was confused by my inability to get so much as a job interview. 'Something strange is taking place and I don't know what it is,' he warned me. If any senior officers were doing something to justify my paranoia, he didn't know about it. Although he was one of the top twenty officers in the Metropolitan Police, if a group had plans to undermine me, he wasn't privy to that information. He wasn't one of them.

AC Ghaffur didn't back off my case. He showed my file to the commissioner, Sir John Stevens, who had replaced Sir Paul at the top of the Met. It made little difference: Chief Supt Otter wasn't going to support any applications for a promotion, and I was trapped at Kensington. When I represented PC Joy Hendricks, a black officer who had been taunted about her colour, given a present of white face paint, and called 'Stevie Lawrence number two' by her fellow officer, in a tribunal on 1 June as part of my NBPA work, Chief Supt Otter wasn't pleased. I was losing focus, he said, becoming a maverick.

I was disloyal, he added.

PC Joy Hendricks has since settled her case, receiving £500,000 in compensation.

Bringing this to the attention of a tribunal as part of my job is not, in my opinion, either maverick or disloyal. Many officers could have supported PC Hendricks before the case got to a tribunal. If they don't, out of loyalty, what exactly are they being 'loyal' to?

At the end of June, AC Ghaffur told me there was a job going in Marylebone. It wasn't a promotion, just a superintendent job, but it was in a prestigious area which was under his command. It would have given me my command experience as recommended in my EI assessment. He inquired, and was told that if I wanted it, I couldn't have it.

'They've really got it in for you,' he told me on the phone, confused.

Whoever 'they' were, I couldn't fight them. I started to take days off work to go to NBPA meetings and did not claim expenses for them. I wrote my speeches at home, and did the paperwork there, even though I was entitled to do them at the office. I purposely under-claimed my phone expenses, took short lunch hours, and logged all of this behaviour in case 'they' came to get me, and stopped me from going on the Senior Command Course, which was my ticket out of Kensington, and my chance for a fresh start. I just didn't want any more trouble. My file had been passed to the deputy commissioner, so perhaps there would be an opportunity to put my point of view and get a transfer after all; he was going to arrange a meeting with a neutral observer, Sir Herman Ouseley, who was chairman of the Commission for Racial Equality. He seemed like a good choice. Maybe things would work out after all. When we met, on 22 September 2000 at New Scotland Yard, I was delighted. Sir Herman and DAC Orde were both there. DAC Orde admitted I had a point when I presented my evidence, and asked me what I wanted to do about it. I told them that I wanted Chief Supt Otter investigated, that I wanted an apology, and that I wanted the Met to admit its mistakes and learn from them. DAC Orde offered me a secondment with the Serious Crimes Group, to broaden my experience.

I was adamant, but I thought I had a good case. They seemed to agree, but someone didn't. I didn't get my apology, no one's actions would be investigated, and I couldn't go on secondment. The fanatical zeal with which the Met was keeping me in Kensington was wearing me out. I was doing two jobs, one in the office and one at home, as well as trying to protect myself from the consequences of the trouble that both were causing. I tried to make an appointment with Deputy Commissioner Ian Blair, who I knew from my days in Thames Valley. He was now the man with the ability to solve all the problems. The meeting was set for 5 December. I was tired, aggravated and at the end of my patience, which had been stretched further than ever before. Soon, it would snap.

On 5 December, I went to my showdown with DC Blair. After waiting for him for twenty minutes, I heard that it had been cancelled. His secretary booked another meeting for 11 December. That got cancelled. I waited for the next appointment.

I thought I had set in train a sequence of events that would, at best, result in me getting my promotion, or at least a transfer, before going on the command course. At worst, I would be taking my employers to a tribunal, one more black police officer with a grievance that had spiralled out of control.

What I didn't know was that on 6 September, I had unwittingly initiated a completely different set of events that would end up with me in the dock, facing a prison sentence. On that day, my car was scratched. From then, things were never going to 'work out'.

If Chief Supt Otter wasn't at the station, I felt I could go to NBPA meetings without an argument. I was sneaking off like a naughty child, not telling him and not noting the exact reason for the meeting in my diary, just that I was out on business.

On 6 September, I decided to make a spot inspection at Chelsea police station before a lunchtime meeting at Kensington police station. I had been told that I wasn't spending enough time there, so this was a chance to improve that part of my job. There weren't any of my inspectors at the station, so I drove back to Kensington and parked at Cope Place, a road opposite the station, where I found a spot.

That afternoon, I had an NBPA meeting in Pimlico, several

miles away. Chief Supt Otter was on holiday, so I knew I could attend without getting into an argument first. At about 1.30 pm, I walked out of the police station to find that my car had been scratched, deeply, around the entire paintwork. The scratches were obviously vandalism, but were done with a very sharp, fine tool, and the car would need a new paint job in the body shop. I was upset and angry, as Ellie found out when I called her to let off steam.

I wasn't thinking about reporting the incident as a crime. I was thinking about how this would play out with Chief Supt Otter. Was I just seeking attention, making trouble, blowing up every incident into a race crime? It might look as if I was making a fuss because I was sulking about not being able to park in the station yard any more. And I would be hard pressed to report it at that point, and still make it to the NBPA meeting that I hadn't told the Chief Supt about, and that he wouldn't want me to attend.

I jumped in the car, and after thirty minutes of ranting on the phone to Ellie I parked it in a road called Emperors Gate, near my gym and close to Gloucester Road tube station, and where I could use my parking permit. I hopped on the tube for the last short part of the journey to my meeting. At the meeting, I heard another of my NBPA colleagues had had his car scratched, so he couldn't make the meeting. I thought about it afterwards: maybe the incidents were connected. I decided to report the damage when I got back to the station, and hopped on the tube to find my car. When I got back to it, I looked again at the damage while I called my mobile phone voicemail. It was vicious.

This sort of crime is so common, sadly, that it barely causes a flicker of interest among police officers, who have seen thousands of scratched or damaged cars. When I reported it, I got a shock. The detective chief inspector leapt into action. He wanted the car photographed, he said, he wanted video recordings of the damage, a crime scene team to look for forensic evidence and house-to-house inquiries.

Oh dear, I thought, I should have reported this three hours ago. If I admitted that, he'd ask why I didn't, and I'd have to tell him that I sneaked off to an NBPA meeting, and that would raise the question of whether I should have reported a crime first or whether I preferred to go to a meeting of black police officers and indulge my maverick obsession with racism, when my commanding officer had told me to spend more time in my operational job.

So, looking for a quiet life, I lied.

'It has been in Cope Place all day,' I said, when the officers asked where the car had been, expecting at that time a bit of paperwork would close the case.

Instead, the road was closed. Twenty police officers fanned out to investigate. Large yellow boards appealing for information were set up. A detective inspector was given the case to investigate. AC Johnston rang to commiserate, as did Chief Supt Otter, calling in from his holiday.

Did I want to report this as a race crime? No, I said, there's no evidence that's the case, and I wasn't in the car at the time, but two hours later it was classified that way anyway. AC Ghaffur had received some hate mail that day, so the theory was that two scratched cars plus hate mail in one day might be a pattern of abuse, perhaps from an unhappy police officer who nursed a grudge.

No culprit was ever found. No member of the public had noticed my car being scratched, no one came forward with information based on the big yellow signs. It's hardly surprising. Cars get damaged all the time, and this one was investigated like a murder. I was surprised, but had other things on my mind, and I thought little about the embarrassing lie I had told.

How do I know so much detail about the events of that afternoon? Because I read all about it in surveillance logs. By the time my car was scratched, I had been under covert investigation for one year, by members of my own force.

I didn't know who 'they' were when AC Ghaffur mentioned that they were out to get me – but in the three years following 6 September 2000, I would find out. The surveillance teams of Operation Helios, the covert investigation into my supposed criminality, was logging every move I made, every email I sent, recording every call at work and translating and transcribing it. Eventually I would be able to make sense of the ridiculous things that kept happening to me during 2000, but only when I was sent for trial and saw the innocent details of my life twisted into evidence that I was a common criminal.

4 Under suspicion

In October 1998, a police informant in Thames Valley mentioned that a police officer called Ali could fix speeding tickets, for a price.

I was also regularly snorting cocaine, he said.

Not that he knew me himself, he admitted. He'd heard it through the grapevine. It was a throwaway comment. It wasn't relevant to the job he was being paid to do.

If you're my boss, there are three ways to deal with this sort of accusation. You might decide it is nonsense. Police officers can't fix speeding tickets, and you know this – because the system is computerised and they don't have access to the computer. Speeding tickets are computer generated by speed cameras! Or, you could serve me with a Reg 9 and ask if I can explain myself, so at least I know what I have been accused of.

Or you order a covert investigation into my conduct and put a note on my record without telling me – whether or not you find the accusation had any substance.

In 1998, if someone had told me about this informant and his active imagination, the next five years might have been different. Handling informants is a subtle job. On one hand, they are essential links to the criminal world. On the other, they are by definition untrustworthy, whichever side of the law you're on. There's also the problem that the more they can tell their handler, the more status they have, the more respect they get – and the more money they will receive. The temptation for informants to dress up rumour as fact, or to simply create their own stories, is well known to any cop with any common sense.

You have to treat any information that an informant discloses with caution, especially when it's against a fellow officer. There's a process for dealing with a complaint: you ask the informant to make a statement. You tell the officer that a complaint has been made, and issue a Reg 9.

At times, there are reasons to keep internal corruption investigations covert, the most important being that the officer being investigated might be able to cover his tracks. We know from experience that corrupt officers are, by nature, clever people who are only too aware of what the police can do. They take precautions, and therefore an investigation into their conduct needs to be as sophisticated as they are.

There is also one very good reason not to keep the investigation secret: specifically, that by bringing the subject up, you could sort the whole thing out very quickly. In this case, I could have pointed out that it is almost impossible to 'disappear' a parking ticket. There is a record that they were issued, a record that they have been paid, and neither is the responsibility of a police inspector working at his police force's headquarters, which was where I was stationed at the time. Five minutes would have taken care of that. It would have taken even less time to deal with the drug taking: I would have volunteered for a test, at any time.

At Thames Valley, no one considered there was any need for an investigation at the time, because it was obvious the complaint was barmy. I didn't know it existed. It was noted, and forgotten.

In December 1998, the National Criminal Intelligence Service let Thames Valley Police know that someone I knew was suspected of being involved in drug distribution. It's a serious charge, but again, I didn't know about it. As a police officer, it's quite reasonable that you're not expected to hang around with drug dealers; but at the same time, you are not permitted to use the police national computer to look up the files of people you know unless there's a legitimate reason to do it. If I was ever in the company of a drug dealer, I didn't know about it.

When I transferred to the Met, someone decided to pass on these two nuggets of intelligence, perhaps out of concern, or perhaps out of spite. During Operation Helios, CIB3 took a statement from Sir Paul Condon who – to their disappointment – said he knew of this accusation but still decided to offer me a job, since it was baseless. Clearly not everyone agreed with him.

In 1999, soon after I joined the Met, someone called Crimestoppers, the anonymous telephone service, to tell the operator that I was a burglar. No one had mentioned any of this to me, probably because this sort of intelligence is routine. If you are a black officer, frequently in the media talking about racism, it is sadly inevitable that you attract all sorts of malicious complaints.

When I first joined the police it wasn't unusual to be called a Paki or 'Ayatollah' to my face. Nowadays racists are smarter: they would be foolish to call a black or Asian police officer racist names. It is easier to leave an anonymous message on the Crimestoppers telephone service that I was a burglar.

And if you live in London and know a lot of people, you probably know someone who either has a criminal record or has been investigated. It's a fact of life, but you don't necessarily know about it. People don't normally advertise their criminal records. To the police, the person is of suspect character, possibly engaged in criminal acts. To you, the same person is that guy you met the other night, or the friend of a friend you met over dinner.

Armed with this information, someone made the surprising decision that the best course of action would be to tap my phone at work and place me under surveillance. The decision to initiate covert surveillance is a big step, because it implies that the trust between the Met and me had broken down, only a few months after I joined. Someone was genuinely concerned that I wasn't just undermining my employer, I was also committing crimes

– concerned enough to listen to my telephone calls and to check every parking ticket that I had ever had any involvement with in Thames Valley.

This was Operation Bittern, named after a wading bird with a loud voice. The male bittern, I discovered, is known for having many mates. Perhaps someone was having a little joke behind my back. As I was preparing for EI and wrestling with the problems of parking my car, wearing the wrong belt and being called a fucking tosser at work, my fellow officers were listening, logging and transcribing my calls, and later following me around London.

On 18 August 1999, we know the Bittern team received authorisation from a Metropolitan Police commander for four weeks of Private Side Intercept – a tap – on my work telephone. We also know that a surveillance team of thirteen officers followed me and logged my movements. The permission was extended when the officers involved presented evidence that it was worth extending the surveillance, which was cancelled on 12 November.

What did Bittern uncover? The officers discovered that my friend, Eddie Parladorio, was associating with two ex-officers who were once investigated because they were wrongly suspected of corruption. This is hardly surprising. Like many solicitors who work for high-profile firms, Eddie had to use private investigators. It was his job. The officers in question had resigned from the police force and become PIs. They had not been convicted of any offence.

They discovered that I tried to resolve the dispute between Ali Ghavami and his builders, by asking the local bobby to call at Mr Ghavami's house for a cup of tea and to reassure him after he had been physically threatened by a builder.

They discovered that, on 24 September, I was associating with a nurse who was supplying me with needles – for my mother. It's another example of how difficult life is in Iran. My mother suffers badly from arthritis, and has to have regular painkilling injections. In Iran, the quality of needles is terrible: they are blunt and used to leave her covered in bruises. When I knew I was going to see my mother, I asked a nurse I knew if she could get me some needles that I could take to Iran for my mother. It's common practice. When Iranians visit home, they stuff their luggage with things that British people take for granted, but which make a huge difference to the quality of life for their families: good soap, shampoo, medicine. Later, this piece of 'evidence' was added to the logs of Operation Helios, with the year taken off; perhaps as an attempt to shore up the increasingly strained story that I was taking drugs during 2000.

By any normal standard, it was dull stuff. There was no evidence of any criminal conduct to sustain Bittern. The best the investigators could come up with was that I was married and yet had other girlfriends. Had they asked, I could have told them that Natalie knew, and fully agreed with our lifestyle. Instead, they assumed that I was seeing other women behind my wife's back. This was probably not what parliament intended when it passed legislation allowing police to conduct surveillance on career criminals about to commit serious crime.

Even if I had been having a clandestine affair behind my wife's back, it wouldn't have been the first time a police officer had had an affair, and was – frankly – nobody's business but mine unless it affected my conduct in the job.

And that, more or less, was it. A girlfriend, a few phone calls and a friend who's a solicitor is pretty thin stuff if you're trying to establish a pattern of serious criminality. If this is justification for covert surveillance, we're all at risk. There were two more possibilities as to why I was singled out: my fellow officers felt threatened by my opinions, and the fact that I was so eager to voice those opinions. In addition, they were apprehensive that I would soon be promoted and have real influence. Perhaps that, more than a couple of wild accusations about my conduct, is a more credible reason they wanted to find out if there was anything hidden in my private life.

On the other hand, perhaps they really found my behaviour odd, because I didn't behave like them. I wasn't often in the pub with them, I didn't eat with them because I couldn't eat the canteen food, and I didn't share the political views of many of them. The differences between Iranian culture and traditional British ways of doing things were magnified in my job. If a friend who owned a car showroom lent me a valuable car for a couple of days, he wasn't trying to buy special treatment by the law, and he didn't get it. Traditionally, if we have things, we share them. That's not corruption, it's our culture.

The police service needs to face up to the real meaning of diversity. It has to face the fact that if police officers from other cultures join up, they might not see the world the same way that the dominant police culture sees it. Diversity isn't just about colour, it's about different attitudes and ideas as well. The senior officers in the Met also couldn't have it both ways, on one hand recommending me for promotion and at the same time investigating me, but as soon as Bittern started, that's the situation we were in. Not for the first time, I had polarised the opinions of my colleagues. Diversity is not a beauty contest. People are different and alternative ways of life need to be respected. This understanding seemed to be lacking from the Bittern logs.

The worst possible interpretation of Bittern was that in the post-Macpherson atmosphere of resentment someone wanted to learn more about the work we were doing at the NBPA. If that was the case, the best way would be to listen to its legal advisor – me – not least because some people saw me as a subversive. The problem with this was that many of my conversations contained legally privileged information, because it related to legal cases against the police brought by black officers who I represented. Legal privilege has long standing in English law; it is also protected by legislation. It is there to protect lawyers and their clients and representatives, so they can communicate without fear of interference by the police.

Some of our work was threatening for other reasons: we were building alliances with other organisations such as the Society of Black Lawyers and Probation Officers. We were not trying to create a civil rights movement, but simply ensuring that the voice of ethnic minority communities could be heard inside the criminal justice system. This was important because research consistently showed they were disadvantaged as victims and as offenders. At the NBPA, we had constantly heard gossip that some elements were out to undermine us. We don't know if any of those elements had managed to infiltrate Bittern, but if they had, they would have been interested to listen in on my calls. The call logs I have seen certainly show that when they heard about my idea for a solidarity march of black officers in London, similar to the one we had attended in Toronto, they freaked. I'll admit, perhaps British society isn't quite ready yet to see thousands of black police officers marching through its streets. But again we were not trying to imitate the civil rights movement in the US. Our aims were more modest – we thought that a march and show of strength would be the best advertisement for other black people who were thinking about joining the force. Police forces across the country had spent millions in advertisements and had consistently failed to reach their ethnic minority recruitment targets. We were not starting a revolution. We were looking for fresh ways to demonstrate that there is room for ethnic minority officers in the force. It has worked in Canada and the US. It may also work here one day, and then we will have a police service which looks like the community it serves.

On the other hand, the poor Bittern surveillance team must have been bored out of their minds when they discovered the shocking truth about my life. If they were expecting a jet-set lifestyle of bribes and parties, revolutionary politics, sex and drugs, they were disappointed. When they followed me at work, they found that sometimes I would disappear unannounced from the police station, radio in hand. The rather dull reason would be that I was visiting another police station, and had decided to hop on a bus rather than drive. Many police officers dislike taking public transport in uniform, because they feel self-conscious about it. Like my father, I was proud to wear the uniform in public, and didn't change out of it if I was going to walk along the street.

They found me talking animatedly to Middle Eastern people in the street, which they recorded as possible arguments. True, I would often meet Iranians and Arabs, and they would often greet me. When I met Iranians I knew, we would have a conversation in Farsi. Ask an Iranian police officer the time in Farsi and, to an English-speaking Brit, it might look like an argument.

They would sometimes log me wandering the streets around the police station aimlessly, trying to remember where I parked my car because I couldn't put it in the yard.

After work, they could follow me to my gym most nights a week, where I worked out for a couple of hours. They would discover that I liked to eat in my uncle's restaurant, and that sometimes I would bump into people I knew. They would translate my conversations, to find the same dreary mix of domestic arrangements, gossip and chatter that their phone taps would have revealed.

It must have taken hours to draw every conceivable inference so as to conclude that there was criminality taking place. If a friend was leaving 'something in an envelope' for me at the front counter of the police station, they would conclude that it must be cash (rather than two tickets for me to attend the Muslim New Year celebration). I would be a very poor corrupt cop indeed if I asked for my bung to be delivered to my police station and left with the PC at the front counter.

Fast forward eight months to January 2000; I'm feeling under siege at Kensington police station, though I am still Sir Paul's project.

I have passed EI and I am filling in my form for promotion. I'm expecting the same comments from Chief Supt Otter as I had received on my previous form, and though our relationship has been poor professionally, I'm expecting to be out of Kensington soon. A lot of the other officers think there's something not right about me. By their value systems, maybe they are correct, but they have investigated me once behind my back, and found nothing.

When Nahid Darougeh wrote to the Met making serious accusations about me, it was the smoking gun that some of my colleagues had wished for.

Her main grievance wasn't that I was corrupt as a police officer; it was that I had corrupted her daughter Mandy.

I had known Nahid for several months when I met Mandy, who was a student in her early twenties and also Iranian. Mandy and I had a brief relationship. When I met her, she had been diligent and quiet, concentrating on her degree, very much in the shadow of her mother. During the time I knew her, perhaps partly through my influence, she became more independent. When she finished her degree, she told her mother that she didn't want to pursue a professional career, and instead took a job at the Paparazzi café, owned and run by Tony Alam, a friend of mine. Her mother didn't approve, and neither did I. I thought that with her ability and talent, she shouldn't have given up on a professional career so soon. My relationship with both broke down: first with Nahid, then with Mandy, especially after she started to rent a flat that was only 100 yards from Kensington police station, above my uncle's restaurant. We argued on the street: I thought it would undermine me at the station. I also confronted her about things she had said about me to my friend, behind my back.

It was one of those furious, stupid, relationship-ending public arguments that you don't want to have too often but sometimes can't avoid. I jumped in my car and drove off. Later that night, she phoned me and we argued for another twenty minutes, both of us swearing and threatening, before she hung up. She was outside my house, when my arrangement with Natalie was that we would never bring our relationships home. This was the first time that this had become a problem.

A red mist descended. I phoned her three times and ranted into the phone, which was on voicemail. I said some terrible things to her. 'I will take such revenge on you that like a dog you will be sorry. From now on you are dead. You think it's a bluff. I give you an hour and see what I will do to you,' I shouted.

Each call wound me tighter. 'You want war, bitch, you're going to get war. First I will start with your family and then I come to you and your reputation. I will spread all over London that you are a prostitute.'

Of course it wasn't true. I'm ashamed. It was vile, wrong, inexcusable language to use to someone, whatever our differences had been. When the words were read back in court I realised how terribly I had behaved. I'm sorry now. Later Mandy and I met for coffee, patched up our differences and became friends; it's in the police surveillance logs.

We were two people whose relationship had nowhere to go, blaming each other and letting the hurt spiral out of control. Unknown to me, Mandy had kept the messages and at the time had shared them with her mother.

On 28 January 2000, Nahid's letter accusing me of corruption went to the borough commander's office, to Chief Supt Otter. She was interviewed that day, and on 31 January, Supt Norman, DS Wilkinson, one of the officers who had worked on Operation Bittern, and Chief Supt Otter taped Nahid making accusations. They were excited about this information: they did not want to get anything wrong.

They recorded her as she told them that I was a spy for Iran, that I had beaten up the new boyfriend of an ex-girlfriend, and that I had stolen her son's jumper. On 29 January my accusers had already held a meeting chaired by DAC Trotter and agreed that I was a problem for the Met. The PSI was put back on my work telephone, and Operation Helios had begun.

My codename, Mozart, appears in many of the 2,288 statements, 1,670 exhibits, 2,054 documents and 2,196 actions of Operation Helios; many of those actions were taken in the year that it ran in secret, while I had a dim idea that something odd was happening in my life, but no conception of how every movement and call was being monitored. As I was struggling to comprehend why my application for promotion wasn't being considered, why I was denied a transfer, why previously favourable reviews were downgraded, even why my fellow officers had taken to hanging around in the corridor outside my office, a surveillance team had taken up residence across the street.

My conversations were routinely recorded, and translated if necessary – not, it turns out, especially accurately. Up to forty-four officers were involved in Helios, and at this point I stopped being the golden boy (in truth, I hadn't been that in the eyes of many of my colleagues for many months) and became a loose cannon, a rotten apple. Because I was being investigated, dull, meaningless or harmless events became loaded with significance and formed a supposed pattern of criminality that eventually made the front pages, and even later, landed me in the dock.

If you believe that eventually you will face Judgement Day, where you have to account for everything you have done, then believe me, I have had a sneak preview of mine, and it's not a pleasant experience. As well as the phone tap and the surveillance, my emails were read, my work diary was examined. Although the law made it difficult for the investigators to listen to my mobile calls – that level of intrusion requires the home secretary's authority – they examined the phone records to see who I had called, who called me, and for how long we spoke. They used cell site intercepts to follow my movements. My mobile phone was, effectively, a very expensive tracking device. I still don't know whether they actually tapped my home phone and mobile phone. They still do not have to disclose that information to me – but my intuition is that they did.

They looked into my bank accounts, and examined how much I was withdrawing and depositing to see if I had secret accounts. Once, as I stood at an ATM to withdraw money, the surveillance log reports that I possessed a gold Visa card. That means that the officer following me must have been right on my shoulder.

My brother's bank account, my wife's and my father's accounts were all looked at without their knowledge. Who owned my father's flat? When I went for a cup of tea, a surveillance officer watched, as four more waited to follow my car.

Later, the surveillance was stepped up. I was photographed and videoed as I went back and forth from my house. Secret audio recordings were taken. Sadly, they were of such poor quality that the Helios officers needed to send them to the BBC's sound experts to be enhanced, and when they failed, the British secret services were employed for the same task. Secret cameras hidden in shoulder bags videoed me as I ate my dinner in restaurants.

When you're outside, often someone is doing the videoing for you, so Helios officers requested CCTV footage too: recordings of me drawing money from an ATM, and at a tube station. Every cup of coffee I drank in my friends' cafés and restaurants was logged as a gratuity. Chief Supt Otter would have recognised one of the locations, because it was where he and I had eaten a free meal when he persuaded me to join him at Kensington police station.

The logs discovered me visiting the Iranian Embassy, which of course fitted the suspicion that I was a spy. Because this was secret surveillance, they couldn't ask me why I had visited the embassy. I could have told them that I went there once to get visas for my children to visit Iran. Perhaps the fact that I went there in uniform with one of my officers should have shown that there was nothing ominous about the visit. I also went there for a function at Iranian New Year with 500 other expatriates. Officers from the Diplomatic Protection Group were also guests there. But later, one of my Reg 9s referred to my habit of visiting the embassy, and also the Liberian Embassy, without permission, 'with ominous intent'.

When Detective Constable Paul Douglas of Special Branch read about my suspension in the *Guardian*, he thought it odd, because he remembered me. As he wrote in a memo to his boss at Special Branch, 'On each occasion Mr Dizaei telephoned to inform the Iran desk that he was visiting the Iranian Embassy. No written record was kept, but Supt Dizaei is memorable because he is the only superintendent ever to have contacted the reporting officer prior to visiting the Iranian embassy.'

The Helios officers omitted in all their thousands of actions to check whether I had, in fact, obtained permission to visit the embassies before charging me with a disciplinary offence. Although you might think that if they were listening to my phone calls at work, they would have heard, and logged, my calls to the Iran desk. The initial suspicion about my threat to national security had come from Mandy's mother. She apparently decided I was a spy because I knew that her husband was in prison in Iran, which isn't evidence of anything. But by the time Helios was in progress, the initial evidence had been forgotten, and what the officers saw instead was a 'pattern of behaviour'.

As the investigation expanded, the evidence of the logs shows that innocent, everyday behaviour can be interpreted to fit a pattern of supposed criminal wrongdoing. Ellie's mother fell off a bus in November 1999 and suffered permanent injuries. She wanted to claim some compensation, but she couldn't do this without finding out the name of the bus driver. The police who investigated the injury should have provided this information, but had failed to do so – so one night, over dinner, she asked me if I could help.

I was operational superintendent in charge for the area in which the accident took place, so it wasn't hard to do the job that the other officers should have done months previously and find the file to pass to the solicitors. I also gave her the advice that everyone gives to someone who is asking for compensation: don't accept the first offer.

Later, when she accepted a bigger offer, the Helios officers were delighted to hear me jokingly ask Ellie's mother on the phone for my *shirini*. Literally, I'm asking for a sweet pastry. It's a custom in Iran that when you have good luck, buy a new house for example, or get a new job, you give out sweets, so my asking for a *shirini* is roughly equivalent to saying, 'You owe me a beer for that.'

On the other hand, the Helios officers decided I was asking for a cash payment, and questioned Ellie's mother about it later, much to her confusion. As she pointed out, because I helped her, I prevented a formal complaint against the Met from her.

Ellie was unwittingly a central part of the investigation into me. She loves to nag family and friends about the toxic ingredients in food, drugs and supplements. We're all sick of hearing about it. I'd beg her to stop nagging me about it, but she knows what she is talking about, because she is a toxicologist and a senior research fellow into poisons. So one day we were shopping in Kingston-upon-Thames, and Ellie watched in horror as I bought some zinc tablets for £12, which I used to help me train in the gym. Unknown to me, she made a mental note to find out what was in them, and called me the next day.

Ellie   You know those tablets you bought?

Me   The ones from the health shop?

Ellie	Don't take them! They are not good for you, you don't know the side effects.

Me	I paid £12 for them! I'm going to finish them.

Ellie	You know that…

Me (exasperated)	*For God's sake!* Do we have to talk about this on the phone?

This became the evidence that I was taking drugs. Alongside my request for needles for my mother, the conclusion was: I'm on steroids. Since they were checking every transaction on my bank account daily it would not have been hard to see that a few days previously I had purchased an item from Holland and Barrett, a well-known health food shop, for £12.

As the Helios investigators taped and transcribed my calls, they didn't only catch my family and friends in the net: they broke the law. Some of my calls were about NBPA business, and some of those calls were discussions of the tribunal cases in which I represented black officers. The information was private, between the officer and me, in the same way that the police cannot eavesdrop on the conversation between a defendant and his or her solicitor in a criminal case.

On 25 October 2000, I was talking to Eddie Parladorio, my friend who is also a solicitor, to discuss the case of Reheena Siddiqi, who was suing the North Yorkshire force. The recording was tapped, recorded and transcribed – by the police. When I saw the transcript, it made me wonder what else had been transcribed, and what other information the investigating officers had passed on. There was a clear conflict of interest, because during that time I had represented many black officers in cases against the Met.

I asked an interested member of parliament, Peter Bottomley, to table a question in parliament about what had happened, because a minister would be able to demand the information from the Met. He promised to raise the question of whether legally privileged information had been transcribed, which he did on 19 July 2001, to which Home Office Minister John Denham replied:

'The Commissioner of Police of the Metropolis informs me that the practice in relation to calls made by Superintendent Dizaei (prior to 2 October 2000, when Regulation of Investigatory Powers Act 2000 came into force) was that all calls on the Metropolitan police service telephone network were recorded. Those which related to his role as National Black Police Association legal adviser were not transcribed and not passed to the team that is investigating his conduct.'

Which, the evidence shows, wasn't correct: on the erroneous assurance of the commissioner of the Metropolitan Police, the minister misled parliament. My local MP, Boris Johnson, followed up the questions with more of his own, and still the minister assured us that no privileged information had been transcribed. Either the Helios team didn't know the law, or it was recording confidential information that it shouldn't have. Eventually, it resulted in Deputy Commissioner Ian Blair being tasked with appearing on Radio Four to admit that, yes, privileged information had been recorded and transcribed in Operation Helios.

Late in 2000, I notice a new guy is hanging around in the gym whenever I'm there. His name is Billy. Billy likes to engage me in idle chat, which to be honest is distracting and irritating. Every day I go to the gym changing room, there he is in his big sweatshirt. Every time I work out, there he is again, trying to chat, still in his sweatshirt.

I didn't know what to make of Billy, who was beginning to get on my nerves. He was odd, because he didn't seem to pick up on my obvious hints that I wasn't interested in talking to him. Then I decided that maybe he was gay, and flattered myself that he must be interested in me. His behaviour was beginning to concern me, as he was almost stalking me. I even bumped into him once in a small and quite obscure Iranian café when I stopped in to pick up some food. He wasn't Iranian, and so there really wasn't much reason for him to be there. But there he was.

One day, Billy introduces a new topic of conversation. He has just bought a dodgy car, he tells me. He suspects the seller. What should he do? 'Get a lawyer,' I said, and that was that.

Unknown to me, I had passed an integrity test. Billy was an undercover police officer, recruited from the West Midlands police force to lure me into admitting my criminality. His job was to make friends with me and draw me out. His bulky sweatshirt hid a microphone, so he could capture the moment. For two months I was subjected to his inane banter, until the investigators presumably gave up and sent him back to the Midlands.

If I had no idea at the time that Billy was a plant, I had even less idea that I had already passed two integrity tests earlier in the year.

One day in the summer of 2000, a Detective Inspector Couch sent the message that he'd like a word with me. Did I know the Liberian ambassador? he asked. I did, I told him, Ali Ghavami and I were good friends.

Mr Ghavami knows Jimmy Sanchez, he told me, and Jimmy Sanchez owned a car that was used in a contract killing. Had I ever met Jimmy Sanchez? I scanned my memory. I honestly had no idea. At a barbecue a few weeks previously, I had been introduced to someone called Jimmy. So I passed this important nugget of information on to DI Couch.

If I did encounter Mr Sanchez, he warned me carefully, *I was not to let him know that he was being investigated.*

DI Couch was wearing a wire, just like Billy. The investigators were primed to record the conversation in which I tipped my criminal associate Jimmy Sanchez off. They followed me to my uncle's restaurant that night. Suspiciously, I went straight to the payphone. Luckily for the Helios team, they had tapped the payphone in my uncle's restaurant. I dialled. They must have been delighted to hear someone answer the phone. This was it:

'How are the kids?' I asked Natalie. I would normally call her on the mobile, but I couldn't get a signal.

I had passed the test – not least because I genuinely had no idea who Jimmy Sanchez was. When the mysterious Mr Sanchez, who lived in Mexico, found out that he was being sought for questioning, he immediately jumped on a flight to London and volunteered a statement that established his innocence.

These two integrity tests were small-time stuff compared to the operation mounted in May and June 2000. It took in the LAPD, the FBI, the DEA, and the Royal Canadian Mounted Police, and gave a couple of Helios officers a nice trip to the US to set it up.

Norman wrote a letter to the FBI and Los Angeles Police Department showing they were planning covert surveillance while I was in Los Angeles to give a speech; an occasion which was later to land me with a disciplinary notice because I had dared to wear my uniform while speaking.

On 12 May, Supt Norman flew to the US to discuss using an undercover officer to trap me. Could I be secretly masterminding an operation to import steroids and fix visa applications? If so, this was the time to find out. He also visited Canada on the trip, because the Royal Canadian Mounted Police had found two Iranian officers who could work undercover in the US. It seems a long way to go, but Helios had also requested help from the

Australian and New Zealand Police in their search for an officer with an Iranian background.

Next, two undercover officers, one male and one female, visited Kensington to become accustomed to the area. They lived in a flat that cost £100,000 a year to rent, had a budget of £150 per day for entertainment, and received an extra £100 per day on their salaries – plus overtime – for the strenuous job of visiting restaurants and being trained in the Met's covert operation procedure.

In November, I attended the conference in Beverly Hills. I was intimidated, because there were lots of well-known people, some Iranians, some not. But my speech went well.

At the coffee break, an Iranian guy came up to me. He was living in Canada, he said, but he'd love to get a visa for the UK. What was Kensington like? I engaged him in a bit of light conversation.

He was trying to sort out some offshore accounts, he said suddenly, how could he lose some surplus cash?

What? I tried to lose him. He followed me around. I told one of the other delegates that this guy was becoming a pest, and devoted a lot of time to trying to avoid him.

In a room nearby, Supt Norman was following the progress of the sting. It wasn't going well, but at least he and a fellow officer had been able to spend a few days in Beverly Hills setting it up, and enjoying the sunshine at a Santa Monica hotel.

Part two of the operation was to introduce the beautiful female who would be a honey trap for me. She never showed. The integrity test was an expensive failure, much like the rest of Operation Helios. But, also like the rest of Helios, you have to admire their inventiveness, even if you feel sorry for their incompetence.

But you can't admire their respect for the rule of law. Later, a report commissioned by the Morris Inquiry showed that Supt

Norman was ignoring the Crown Prosecution Service's advice
that these sting operations may well have been a breach of my
human rights. But he was not going to be put off so easily.

This was police work, not a spy novel. This creativity could have
been tied to something more solid: evidence that I was engaged
in some criminal conduct. There's a reason why investigations
like this don't normally run away, as this one did: there are
constant reviews.

When an investigation could be damaging to the reputation
of the Metropolitan Police, what's known as a 'Gold group' is set
up, a small committee made up of officers and advisors, which
meets occasionally to review the investigation and decide how
it should proceed. The investigating officer lays out the evidence,
and the group makes its decision. There are also regular meetings
with senior officers; those officers steer the investigation, decide
whether or not to pursue lines of inquiry. Finally, outside advisors
such as the Crown Prosecution Service give their advice.

On the other hand, to do that, they have to be in possession
of all the relevant information. And time and again, they
weren't: the Helios files show dates changed and information
left out of briefings. When the advisors gave advice, it should
have been followed. Often, it wasn't.

During 2000, the Helios team wrote a letter to Her Majesty's
Chief Inspector of Schools: could he nominate a colleague in
Ofsted to give an 'objective assessment' of Helios? The inspector
would have to be prepared to 'stand alongside' the Met if Helios
came to press attention. On 18 December 2000, the inspector
returned his report. He notes that not all the information was
shown to him but nevertheless adds, 'If the question is posed,
whether in the Metropolitan Police Service institutional racism
had adversely affected the performance of this officer, the
answer will be yes.'

The Crown Prosecution Service, whose job it would be to

prosecute me on the evidence that Helios discovered, gave its opinion on whether my integrity tests should take place. 'The proposed tests tend to be somewhat contrived, leading to potential challenge,' said the CPS counsel on 24 July, in a letter to the Helios team. Again, on 26 October, another letter confirmed that 'those concerns remain', and also 'reservations about the proportionality of the proposed undercover operation weighed against the suspected offending and the probability of arguments based on article 8 of the Human Rights Convention.' The investigation will inevitably lead to complaints, it added, that those in charge 'were out to get him at all costs.' That reads like pretty clear advice; and yet I was given three separate integrity tests, all of which I passed. Once again it seems someone else was out of control and not me. It takes a very brave senior investigating officer to ignore the advice of CPS in an area of law which is problematic in any event. But once again Supt Norman ignored the consequences.

But looking through the documentation of my case, the most surprising example of a failure to control Helios was a meeting that I nicknamed 'the Windsor summit'. On 5 December 2000, the Met decided that soon I would have to be told about the investigation, and that needed a new strategy: how would it inform the media? How would it change the way I was investigated? Was the investigation fair? What disciplinary charges would be brought against me?

On 20 December 2000, three deputy assistant commissioners, a number of chief superintendents, members of Ofsted, lay advisors and representatives of the Independent Advisory Group and senior members of the Met's Department of Public Affairs led by Chris Webb, its deputy director, checked into twenty-four rooms at a four-star hotel in Windsor, only a few miles from my house in Henley. At a reception that night, over sherry and champagne, they discussed my case, before going to dinner. The next morning, they heard a review of the operation so far by Supt Norman, and then broke into workshops to discuss 'How do we negate the accusation of disproportionality?' Professional facilitators helped to sift the evidence.

Did it give them comfort? When my defence team and I read the minutes of the meeting, it seemed to us that there was an air of desperation. Not surprising: a year had gone by, and they were still not sure whether they even had enough to arrest me.

At the end of the meeting, they decided on a strategy: go for everything. And on 18 January 2001, the day I was suspended, they went for it.

Part four

My days in court

1 Helios in the dock

On 5 July 2002 it was not the first time I had sat in the dock of Court Seven in the Old Bailey. As a trainee barrister, I had taken a course in ethics. We were taken to the Central Criminal Court, and sat in the dock to experience how serious it was to be on trial, while the judge spoke to us about the conduct expected of us when we were prosecuting or defending our cases. Fifteen years later, as I was taken from the cells and led to the dock for real, I understood his words. For the first time, as I was escorted to my place in the dock by a fellow police officer whose job was to guard me, I actually felt like a criminal.

The Central Criminal Court, or the Old Bailey as it is more often known, is the highest-profile criminal court in the country. Trials have been conducted there since 1334, when the courthouse was built on top of London's notorious Newgate prison. The courthouse has been rebuilt several times since, and Newgate prison has long since been closed, but it retains its intimidating history. Prisoners were once led straight from the courtroom to be hanged on the gallows outside, and until 1860 spectators were charged for the ghoulish privilege of attending a 'hanging breakfast'. The prisons emitted such a stench of disease that judges have by tradition carried a 'nosegay' of flowers into court. Above the main entrance, a recording angel is supported by the figures of fortitude and truth. The disease, the stench and the gallows may have gone, but it's not a pleasant place to be when you're accused of a crime.

Court Seven is modern and not filled with elaborately carved wood, peeling paint and stained glass, like some of the show courts. But it did have one very old, very intimidating feature: it was the court of His Honour Judge Sir Michael Hyam QC, the City Recorder. As Recorder of London, Judge Hyam was the most senior criminal judge in the country. I might have been accused of fiddling expenses and lying about the location of a scratched car when the Old Bailey is more famous for trying murderers and rapists, but it seems my case wasn't going to be tucked away in a minor court.

For security reasons, the dock, where the accused sits, is surrounded by a high glass box. It is like sitting in a fish tank. Next to me sat the dock officer. To my right, the jury box, and to my left, the viewing gallery. You don't have to pay admission to get access to the Old Bailey any more; anyone who is interested can walk in off the street to see the entertainment. Directly facing me was Judge Hyam, behind him the royal coat of arms of the United Kingdom, reading 'Honi soit qui mal y pense' – 'Evil be to him who evil thinks' – and the witness box, separated from my fish tank by rows of benches, where the two legal teams sat.

It's not just the surroundings that intimidate you in a courtroom; there is also the process, which has barely changed since the Old Bailey heard its first trial, the old-fashioned dress of the judge and the barristers, wearing ornamental wigs and gowns that fall off their shoulders and constantly need to be hitched up, and even the use of odd over-formal language: as the judge arrives, for example, we aren't asked to stand, we are asked to 'be upstanding'. The defence barrister doesn't say to the judge, 'You ought to see this evidence', he will say; 'This evidence ought to be before M'lord', as if the judge were not in the room at the time. My training in the law, and many court appearances as a police officer, meant that I knew what I would be facing. When it is you who is being referred to as 'the accused', also as if you were not in the room instead of sitting silently fifteen feet away, it's a different story.

My first day in court was not in front of a jury. Instead, my barristers had come to argue that the case against me should simply be dismissed. Today, we would argue points of law.

Luckily, I had a legal team that wasn't about to be intimidated by the Old Bailey and Judge Hyam, as I was. Leading my defence was Michael Mansfield QC, one of the best, and certainly one of the most notorious, criminal defence barristers in the UK. Mansfield was also a long-term and consistent thorn in the side of the police, most recently in the Lawrence Inquiry, where he had represented the Lawrence family. With a flamboyant manner, a long mane of grey hair and well-known anti-establishment views, some considered him a showman, or worse, a publicity-seeking clown who cared less about his cases than about the publicity it would bring him. Having studied the Lawrence Inquiry, I knew though that his flashy exterior concealed a sharp intellect, a devastating technique in cross-examination, and an ability to make a connection with a jury that many posh-sounding, better educated, upper-class barristers simply didn't have.

Getting Mansfield to represent me had not been easy. A few weeks into my suspension, many months previously, the NBPA had written to him to ask him to represent me if the case came to trial. He had agreed, but senior barristers don't come cheap, and neither I nor the NBPA had the funds to pay for his time. My solicitors and the Superintendents' Association both counselled against employing him – they didn't think that the minor accusations against me would get his attention or justify his bill.

First, the money: there was a way to get Michael Mansfield QC on my team without breaking the bank. As I was accused of a criminal offence, under British law I was eligible for legal aid, which meant that the state would pay the costs of my defence. Legal aid was not designed so that everyone could hire senior barristers though, and my solicitors said I simply couldn't get Mansfield. The QC after his name stands for Queen's Counsel – a select group of around 1,000 senior barristers, out of the 14,000 practising in the UK, who have proved themselves the most able in their profession. QCs do not, habitually, defend cases based on scratched cars. Three times I had been told that there would be a decision on when and where I would stand trial, and three times I was told there would be a delay (I later discovered this was due to haggling behind the scenes between the police and the CPS). On 19 December 2001, I was given the Christmas present that nobody wants: a date at the Old Bailey. In the new year, my solicitors delivered the bad news that I would have to make do with a more junior barrister. I barely held on to my temper and stormed out of their offices, straight to the library of the Middle Temple, of which I was still a member following my short and unfulfilled legal career. I was determined to prove them wrong.

When I looked at the law, I was convinced they were wrong. I was entitled to a QC under legal aid, simply because of the stature of the legal team against me, which was being led by a prosecuting barrister known as a Treasury Counsel – an even more rarefied group nicknamed the 'devils', hand-picked to prosecute criminal cases in the Central Criminal Court. The barrister who would prosecute me wasn't just a Treasury Counsel, but one of eight Senior Treasury Counsels. He wasn't just one of the eight, either – since 1 April 2002, Richard Horwell, prosecuting, had been the First Senior Treasury Counsel to the Crown. If QCs don't defend cases involving scratched cars, it must be the first and will probably be the last time that the First Senior Treasury Counsel has prosecuted one.

The Human Rights Act 1998, Article 6, said I was entitled to a fair trial and that meant adhering to a principle known as 'equality of arms'. This meant that the junior barrister appointed to defend me wouldn't do. In court, I worried he'd be eaten alive by the first senior devil.

I knew Mansfield wasn't going to be eaten up by anybody on the opposing team. His ordinary middle-class upbringing was unexceptional – except for his parents, who were firm believers in the principle of right and wrong. As a boy, he had witnessed his mother going to court to overturn a parking ticket given to her in error, and watched as the police officer lied in court to protect himself. 'If men in uniform can do this,' his mother told him, 'what else is going on in the world?'

Barristers come in pairs: I thought Mansfield would work better when he was supported by a junior who was a 'copper's barrister', someone who was accustomed to being on the side of the police. So I asked for Michael Egan, another barrister who had made a name for himself at the Lawrence Inquiry when he was on the opposite side to Mansfield. At the Lawrence Inquiry, he had the hopeless task of defending the police investigation, but had been brave enough to do the unpleasant but necessary job of cross-examining the victim's mother. No one could accuse him of being a woolly liberal, or a police-hater, two insults routinely lobbed at Mansfield. I didn't know if he would like me, but I knew that I needed someone on my side who would disagree, and question our assumptions, and be able to empathise with the case against me.

At 9–12 Bell Yard, Egan's chambers, the other barristers had a good laugh at him when he was asked to be Mansfield's junior. But, despite the obvious problems, he agreed.

Mansfield admitted to me that when he saw Egan was going to be his junior, he was 'surprised about the choice'. Mansfield had a reputation for criticising the establishment, and he was working with a team of police solicitors, and a junior who was noted for defending white officers in court who were accused of racism. The last time they had met professionally was during the public inquiry into Stephen Lawrence's murder, when they had been on opposing sides. Mansfield and Egan had different ideas about the trial, but the opposite to what you might expect. Mansfield wanted to fight the case purely on the law. Egan wanted to accuse the Met of a racist witch-hunt. As the trial progressed, the good-natured tension between their contrasting styles was to help all of us.

I liked Mansfield immediately, and enjoyed meetings with him, where he would wear his tracksuit rather than a stiff collar. I liked his easy-going manner and fondness for a beer, but professionally he worried me slightly. It seemed he was a bit too easy-going. He admitted he had never expected to see me in his office, because he was certain the case would never reach court. I fretted that this meant he wasn't going to be ready for a trial – but my solicitor, Ian Lewis, reassured me that when it was the right moment, Mansfield would get stuck in. With material arriving from CIB once a fortnight, there were literally hundreds of folders of evidence to look at. Luckily, I had nothing better to do than to look at them.

When you're prosecuted for an offence, you are allowed to see the evidence that will be used against you, so that your barrister can defend you. It's a principle of a fair trial: while the state can investigate you without telling you, if the prosecution was allowed to ambush you in court, then it would be impossible to refute the evidence against you at that time – even if you could refute it later. The process of handing over the information used to build a case against you is called 'discovery', and it would be vital in my case.

Under the terms of the Criminal Procedure and Investigations Act 1996, any major investigation has a 'disclosure officer' – in my case DS Fox – whose job was to hand over all the relevant documents at the earliest possible time, to give the defence barrister the opportunity to build a case. This is called 'primary disclosure'. When the defence outlines its strategy, before trial, it triggers 'secondary disclosure' – that is, any further information that might be relevant to its case.

In the real world, the disclosure process is rarely as perfect as that. The prosecution will sometimes supply only the information that is strictly relevant, or on occasions will supply hundreds of pages of information, hoping to bury the flaws in a weak argument. Sometimes they will drag out the process, bending the rules slightly. And there's no need for the police to tell you why the information they have used is relevant to their case: just that it is relevant. Trying to construct a meaning from the roomful of detailed, shocking, embarrassing and often bizarre information that arrived on my doorstep was frustrating and numbing, more so because the telephone transcripts were of my personal calls, the investigations were into the private lives of my friends and colleagues, and the life laid out in their reports was mine – or at least, a strange distortion of mine.

One of the clues buried in our disclosure papers had brought us to court in July 2002. Why had officers been instructed to find out when I was sworn in as a constable in Thames Valley? The law states that to act as a police constable, I had to be sworn in by a magistrate, which I was. Later, there was a statement from a chief inspector in Thames Valley, who told CIB I had ceased to be a constable on 29 March 1999, when I had transferred to the Met. What on earth were they investigating?

And then it dawned: the Police Act of 1996 means that I had not legally been a police officer for my entire Metropolitan Police career. The Met has its own rules for swearing in constables – you have to be sworn in by an assistant commissioner, which never happened in my case. I was being prosecuted for misconduct in public office, but I had never legally been in public office when the misconduct occurred.

It was a legal trick, but I needed every trick I could find. Mansfield didn't think it would work, but he agreed to give it a go. That's why I was in the dock in Court Seven, desperately hoping that I could escape on a technicality, and all this would simply go away. It didn't. The prosecution didn't even bother sending

Horwell, the Senior Treasury Counsel: that was how seriously
they took our legal argument. Judge Hyam agreed. Application
dismissed: I had lied about the location of my car, and that was
enough to send me to trial. I would be back in court on 6 January
2003, this time to be tried before a jury. If I lost, I could face a
hefty prison term. If I was to avoid having my entire career and
private life exposed to ridicule in court, and worse, being locked
up as a criminal afterwards, we had to put the whole Helios
process on trial.

The last effort we could make to avoid a court case was what is
known as an 'abuse' application. Basically, this means that we
believed the investigation into my supposed criminal conduct
wasn't done in good faith: that because the entire point of Helios
was to find me guilty of something, I couldn't get a fair trial. It
was the first time that Mansfield and Egan decided to make a
point of my race, to suggest – as seemed clear to us from the
details of Helios which had been released – that the investigation
had a racist motivation. Simply put, if I hadn't been from another
culture, I wouldn't have been treated with such suspicion and
hostility by the Helios investigators. Even more simply put: it was
a witch-hunt.

Egan had spotted what he thought was the most damning
evidence: the letter from Supt Norman to the FBI, suggesting
the sting in Los Angeles. Norman's error, in Egan's view, was
to suggest that this would be the last chance to catch me in a
sting. This sat alongside Supt Russell's letter to the DEA, claiming evidence that I was a drug trafficker. As you recall, that
evidence was a phone call to an ex-partner in which I asked
for some needles to take to Iran; and an argument with Ellie
about vitamin pills. You might also recall that Supt Russell was
appointed to be my superintendent friend immediately after my
suspension.

There was other evidence. 'Even if he doesn't do anything, it will be fatal to his career,' the scriptwriter who had developed my entrapment scenarios had written.

The entire 'Windsor summit' was not exactly standard practice, even if there was evidence against me that was serious.

During this time I would obsessively look over the evidence time and again, searching for a chink of light, some mistake or error which would give me some hope. One evening at 9 pm, a few weeks before the abuse hearing, I found it. I called my solicitor, Ian Lewis.

'Have you read this bundle?' I asked him. He confirmed he had, but hadn't noticed anything odd in there.

'It's not what is in there,' I told him, 'it's what is missing.'

The Met's Independent Advisory Group officers were at the Windsor summit. It was CIB3's job to keep them informed about all the significant features of the investigation, so that they could make a judgement on how reasonable the investigation was. The integrity tests were certainly significant, in their cost if not in the results they achieved. There was not one mention of the attempted entrapment in Los Angeles, by 'friend' Billy from the gym, or my fellow officer feeding me with information in the hope that I would pass it on to Ali Ghavami, the Liberian ambassador, who later complained of unnecessary police attention.

The point was, I had passed all these integrity tests, and there had been more planned. Had they been discussed at that time with the IAG, then CIB3 might have been told that enough was enough. They were not discussed, I pointed out to Lewis.

I believed that my accusers were handling the IAG to make a case that I had been investigated fairly – even if this meant skipping over some of the important details.

This dragged on through the rest of 2002. Christmas was not happy in my house. For the second Christmas in a row I had to face my family, knowing that this might be my last with them for several years. My kids were ill. They asked me if their dad was going to jail. I couldn't answer, because I didn't know, and I couldn't find the words to comfort them. Not for the first time, Natalie was the strong one. She took the responsibility, because the enormity of what might happen after Christmas left me lost for words.

Abuse arguments generally take a day in court. There is no jury, and rarely any witnesses. It's a legal argument between barristers, based on a small portion of evidence, with a judge making a decision. Ours took five weeks.

Mansfield was on home territory. He listed all the reasons why the investigation was flawed: the letter to the FBI, the letter to the DEA, the Windsor summit and the IAG…it was a long list.

The prosecution, to repudiate his points, called the newly promoted Chief Supt Norman as a witness. This had become a trial within a trial. My biggest chance of being found not guilty seemed to be in having the case thrown out before it began. That relied on Mansfield making Chief Supt Norman concede the abuse argument in front of the judge, so that the judge would decide in my favour before anything was put in front of a jury.

I was hardly objective, but it seemed to me, and to most of the others in court to help me, that Chief Supt Norman had been put in the witness box to take a verbal pounding from Mansfield. I admit this was a source of great pleasure to me.

On the other hand, the pleasure would be empty if the argument didn't succeed, so at each step, I was looking for anything that would help us. When Mansfield wrung an apology out of Chief Supt Norman over how he had illegally taped and transcribed legally privileged conversations, Chief Supt Norman admitted, under examination by Mansfield, that he had not clearly understood the full implications of legal professional privilege in this context.

I was delighted. When Chief Supt Norman claimed that his 'grammar' had been the source of the error in the letter to the FBI, I was ecstatic. Each 'sorry', each time he said, 'I got it wrong', I listed in a notebook that I took into court every day.

When Mansfield pointed out that in the case notes, the dates of telephone conversations had been fudged to present them as 'fresh information', and a reason to continue the investigation, I could have punched the air. Nothing, however, was as damning as Mansfield's challenge to Public Interest Immunity being used to cover up evidence.

Public Interest Immunity is an essential part of the police's armoury when they make an important case. PII allows the CPS to withhold evidence from the court, and from the defence, because to offer it would be a threat to the public interest. If, for example, it compromised another investigation, or if there was a threat to national security, then PII would be invoked, and the judge would make the decision based on the merits of the case.

That's the theory. In the grubbier world of the courtroom, PII orders are often granted without fully weighing the evidence, because to do so is impractical, if not impossible. Defence barristers, or the accused, are not allowed to see or to challenge the evidence, for exactly the reason the PII order is being sought. The judge is often presented with a mountain of complex evidence, linking to other suspects or cases, which may or may not be significant – indeed, granting the PII order may be the only way to find out if that evidence has the value that is attached to it. The risk of not granting a PII request may be huge, and it's a brave judge that turns one down. In real life, they are often granted virtually on the nod, and though they can be challenged by the defendant's barrister, they are rarely overturned.

Large sections of evidence were subject to PII restrictions. We suspected that this had less to do with my threat to national security than with a desire, conscious or not, to 'tidy up' the evidence and keep inconvenient facts out of the courtroom. On one point, Mansfield decided to challenge the PII protection which was being given.

A name had been removed from a set of applications that

Chief Supt Norman had made for surveillance and phone taps. The applications were significant: they were the forms he had filled in to get permission to tap my phone, and to tail me, even in the US. In the applications, I was an 'associate' of someone who was suspected of a fraud of several million pounds. We didn't know who this could be, but because the mysteriously redacted name played such a prominent part in my investigation, Mansfield decided to find out. He challenged the judge to force the prosecution to reveal the name.

The judge retired to his chambers to decide. And, indeed, to look the name up for himself. He must have had a bit of a shock: the man under suspicion was not some petty criminal or underworld kingpin.

On his return, he told a surprised prosecution team that he would allow Mansfield's challenge. We could see who the mystery suspect was: it was Babak Emamian, the chair of the British Iranian Business Association, a bastion of British values, a supporter of its aims, and a body whose president is Lord Temple-Morris, a barrister who everyone in the court would know by reputation – and quite a few would know personally.

My link with BIBA: it was on BIBA's request that I went to the US to speak.

I had recently argued with Emamian. He was in regular contact with Chief Supt Norman. He took the view that as he had nothing to hide, he should cooperate as fully as possible with the investigation into me. He wanted to help, and would meet the investigators in hotels or at the Institute of Directors, plead my case, and also make a case for BIBA's legitimacy and probity.

I was worried that the conversations would somehow be used to gather material that could be twisted to work against us. The evidence in front of us showed that unfortunately, I had been correct.

CIB3 were primarily interested in Emamian because of the transcript of a telephone call between him and me when we were planning my US trip. We were joking with each other. He told me I should be grateful to be invited to the US. I bragged that he should be grateful to have a senior police officer to legitimise his association. They were silly comments: two guys trying to outdo each other and show off.

For Chief Supt Norman, the conversation could imply that I was legitimising a fraud that was about to go down when I was in the US. That could form the basis of his request to the FBI, the DEA and the Royal Canadian Mounted Police. That could then set in motion the sting operation while I was there. We can't know how seriously he thought that I was about to commit a major fraud. If he honestly thought I was about to commit a serious crime in cahoots with Emamian, he was disappointed. Supt Norman certainly had a creative imagination.

Taking Emamian's name out of the evidence using PII meant that we could not follow this tenuous trail of evidence. By removing his name, the suspicion against me looked serious. Without the fig leaf of PII it was at best tenuous.

Armed with a name, Mansfield questioned Chief Supt Norman about the basis for the so-called fraud. Chief Supt Norman told the court that Emamian had gone through a divorce, and had wanted to hide the details of a bonus from his wife. He asked his bank if he could do this. The bank, not surprisingly, said no.

Under the UK's banking laws, the bank had to mention to the police that Emamian had wanted to 'hide' a large amount of money. It was clumsy, and his ex-wife would have taken a view that he was certainly guilty of something, but in law he had simply asked a question and been given an answer. There was never any question that the money was his, that it was legitimately earned and he never tried to 'hide' it anywhere else.

Had Chief Supt Norman embellished the evidence to justify his case? One important fact suggests he had: this had taken place four years previously, when I was an inspector in the Thames Valley. At the time, I didn't even know Emamian.

Mansfield weighed in: 'Why would you say this was a recent event?' he asked. 'So is Mr Emamian actually a fraudster?'

Chief Supt Norman admitted that, on reflection, he wasn't. 'Have you arrested Lord Temple-Morris then?' Mansfield asked, turning to the bench to add, 'Someone that your lordship will know very well.'

No, he hadn't. 'So is BIBA a fraudulent organisation or not?' Mansfield continued.

No, it wasn't.

'So if it was not fraudulent, why did you redact the names?' Mansfield asked.

This time, there was no answer.

Ultimately, this point-scoring was of little use to any of us, because at the end of five weeks, on Thursday 13 March, Judge Hyam decided that there had been no abuse; whatever the flaws of the investigation, whatever names had been redacted and why, whatever mistakes Chief Supt Norman had made in his grammar, whatever the independent advisors had or had not been told, no longer mattered. The investigation, in the opinion of the court, was fair. I would shortly stand trial in Court Seven of the Central Criminal Court. When Judge Hyam gave Helios a clean bill of health, I noted that Chief Supt Norman almost skipped out of the courtroom, as if I had already been convicted.

I was devastated. CIB3 celebrated outside court. I had lost far more than the first round. Operation Helios had been given a clean bill of health by one of the UK's most senior judges. The following Monday I was due in court to face charges. I was to stand trial on a case that hinged on the simple fact that I had lied about the location of my car when it was scratched.

All we had to offer in my defence was some sort of justification for why I had lied on the day, and to hope that we did a better job than the prosecution.

2   **For the prosecution**

It's Friday 14 March 2003, and I'm back at the Old Bailey. The previous day, the judge had ruled against my abuse application, and on Monday I was going on trial.

With me: my barristers Michael Mansfield and Michael Egan, and my solicitors, Ian Lewis and Sadiq Khan, who is now a Labour MP. It was time to talk about tactics for the trial, although with the tools at our disposal, tactics is a strong word for what we could do.

Most of the possible avenues for me had already been closed off. In the pre-trial hearing, Mansfield had asked Chief Supt Norman why CIB3 considered me a threat to national security. He had a source, Chief Supt Norman had said. When Mansfield asked who the source was, my accusers had pleaded Public Interest Immunity. The judge had granted it.

In a moment, that had ruled out any reference to Helios at my trial. If any witness from CIB3 was asked about the investigation, they could answer that I was a threat to national security, but they could not disclose why, to protect their source. It wouldn't look good in front of the jury. An Iranian Muslim plus a threat to national security: this combination would not appeal to many jurors.

The judge had made one exception: it was admissible to say I was under surveillance. It would be perfectly legitimate for the prosecution to introduce my recorded telephone conversations, and logs of when and where I was when I was being followed by a fourteen-man surveillance team, as evidence for a trial based on the location of a scratched car, without giving a detailed explanation why. It would not take a very imaginative jury to infer that I must be guilty of something: police officers are not routinely investigated like this. Again, it didn't look good. I felt I was fighting my case in handcuffs.

And that's why, on the afternoon of the Friday before my trial, Mansfield offered me three choices, none of which I wanted to take.

'You could make a protest appearance,' he offered. This involved going to court, saying nothing, offering no real defence, almost certainly being found guilty, and taking my chances on a more sympathetic hearing on appeal, when Mansfield could argue that relevant evidence had been excluded from my trial. This was the option Mansfield seemed to prefer, although he didn't say as much. It offered the chance that at some time in the future, I would be exonerated. For a few minutes, I agreed. But then the frightening reality of what would happen to me if I took this course became obvious. I would go to prison. By the time my appeal was heard, I might have been there for two years. No one has a good time in jail, but former police officers have a worse time than most, and I was scared. The protest appearance may have been the percentage decision: I wasn't brave enough to play the percentages.

The other two options were to try to sneak in a mention of Helios through the back door. If it went well, Mansfield explained, we could win the sympathy of the jury by letting them glimpse the scale of the investigation that surrounded me. But mentioning Helios would immediately provoke the prosecution to mention my supposed threat to national security. Any sympathy the jury had for me would be countered by the strong suspicion that I was a spy, or a terrorist. It was a high-risk strategy, and might be exactly what the prosecution wanted us to do.

The third option looked like my only chance. I wasn't going to fight the charge on its merits – I had lied. The defence was to show the jury that I had lied under pressure, because I didn't know what else to do, and try to convince them that the car was still scratched when it was near the police station. Mansfield thought he could work with this option too. It gave us a chance to do something positive, even if we were boxed in by legal restrictions that would make it harder to explain exactly why I was under so much pressure.

'Don't wear a suit,' Mansfield told me that afternoon. I had taken care to dress up for the abuse hearing, always wearing a suit and tie, but on that Friday I was in casual trousers and a T-shirt, which I preferred. I don't wear a tie unless I have to; out of uniform, I don't feel comfortable dressed like that. That was just fine by Mansfield. He explained: the prosecution case relied on presenting me as a powerful, influential, intimidating figure. If I looked like an ordinary guy, as I did in my casual clothes, it would undermine their argument.

'When the jurors are brought in, sit up straight,' Lewis chided me. First impressions, I knew, really do count in a jury trial. But it's one thing to listen to this advice in a lecture, or hear it in a solicitor's anecdote, and quite another to know in real life that your deportment can help keep you out of prison. On Monday morning, I sat straight.

It helped that I wasn't going to be sitting straight in the fish-tank dock in Court Seven. Instead, the judge allowed me to sit behind my lawyers. Anyone sitting in the dock is separated from the public – in many ways, they already look like a criminal to the jury. Much to the disgust of the prosecution, I got a better seat in court, and one more small advantage.

Today's courtrooms are rarely as neat and tidy as they look in TV dramas. Often, the evidence is stashed in makeshift piles of files; boxes of papers sit on the floor, cupboards that were never designed for holding evidence are pressed into service, laptops sit open behind the barristers, ready to call up any point of evidence or witness statement. My case had literally lorry-loads of evidence, and it couldn't all be brought into court. Much of the prosecution case was stored in a police office building called Jubilee House in Putney, ten miles west, across the centre of London and also in a coded location known as 'Miami', an old police station in Kent.

So on the morning of 17 March 2003, day one of my trial, Court Seven had a strange collection of hangers-on and visitors alongside the usual cast. There were motorcycle couriers ready to climb on their bikes at any time when a valuable document was needed. There were the representatives of CIB3 and the police. In the visitors' gallery, my supporters from the NBPA would gather. Although they couldn't report the trial until it finished, reporters were following it, hoping for a sensational story. Disclosure officers DC Rich and DS Fox were there, in charge of their laptop, which presumably held all sorts of important evidence.

The Central Criminal Court didn't have separate rooms for the two sides to meet, so we both awkwardly crammed into the canteen each day, two rival camps at different ends of the room. Sometimes we'd whisper furtively about our plans for the day. Occasionally we'd sneer across the room at each other, trying to intimidate each other, looking tough. At 8.30 each morning I would meet with my barristers. During the frequent breaks, the officers who supported me would sit down for a cup of tea. Panicky ushers, whose job it was to make sure that everyone who was meant to be in court was there on time, would try and separate the spectators from the participants, which wasn't always easy. The extraordinary thing about this case was that the supporters of both sides, the prosecution and defence, all had one thing in common. We were all officers of the law. The difference that no one could miss was in my camp all the officers were black and on the other all white. We should have been on the same side, working together, but we had picked our sides. We were enemies. The Metropolitan Police had turned on itself.

When the jury was selected, I was delighted to find it had eight members who were either black or Asian with two Muslims. On the far side of the court from me, the prosecution barristers sat unconcerned, confident that they would win. They were still celebrating the failure of our abuse application. You had to agree, their chances looked good.

The legal games, the formality and the obscure jargon of the British court system mask the human cost of the verdicts it produces. I was forced to confront that reality in a way I had never thought about when I was training as a barrister, or giving evidence in court as a police officer. During the early part of my trial, I sat with Natalie in a coffee bar one Saturday afternoon in Windsor High Street. I admitted to her that I was 95 per cent certain that I would be sent to prison if I was convicted.

'What will we do for money when I go to jail?' I asked her, for the first time planning a life for my family when I was behind bars. 'You will have to sell the house.'

'If that happens,' she said, always practical and calm, 'the rest of us can move in with my parents.'

She thought for a while, doing the sums in her head.

'If you are found guilty, will your pay stop right away, or will they give you a month's wages?'

Leading for the Crown Prosecution Service was Richard Horwell, barrister of Hollis Whiteman chambers, appointed to First Senior Treasury Counsel to the Crown at the Central Criminal Court on 1 April 2002. He was a senior barrister with an excellent record and a lot of ability. He also had, in my opinion, a pompous and arrogant manner and seemed determined to make this stupid case seem as important as possible to the jury. In front of him were around twenty lever arch files, with the name 'Ali Dizaei' stencilled carefully on each one. I wondered if he had done it himself, charging by the hour, or had made sure one of the junior barristers at Hollis Whiteman had lettered them carefully for him. He began, as the case proceeded, with an irritating habit of elongating my job title, perhaps to emphasise how senior I must have been, and so how shocking Su-per-in-ten-dent Dizaei's lie was.

In a criminal trial, the prosecution makes its case by calling witnesses. After the prosecution's barristers have examined them, the defence has the opportunity to ask its own questions – that's cross-examination. After the prosecution rests its case, the defence calls its witnesses. I was to be a witness for the defence, but first, the prosecution had many, many witnesses to call.

By the time I spoke in court, it might be too late to help myself. It certainly seemed that way from the witness statements that I was reading. If all the police officers simply came to court and stuck to the language they had used in their statements, I had no chance. Luckily, some of the key witnesses did not.

One of the most damaging early testimonies could have been from Detective Constable Fergus Campbell, based in Notting Hill. I liked him, even if I had trouble fathoming his Scottish accent at times. He was the officer who took the report of damage to my car. The purpose of calling him to court was for the prosecution to show that I was determined to make the scratch on my car into a racial incident, abusing my authority to demand a large-scale investigation. Looking at DC Campbell's statement, he would be one of Mr Horwell's best witnesses. It didn't go quite as the prosecution planned.

Horwell   Mr Campbell, when you saw Mr Dizaei, what did he say to you?

Campbell   He said, 'I want to report the damage to my car.'

Horwell   Who asked for it to be a racial incident?

Campbell   I did.

Horwell (surprised)   Who asked for it to be a racial incident?

Campbell   I did, sir. We have guidelines which say that if a victim of crime is of a different colour and has a high profile, we ought to ask them.

Horwell   And what did he say?

Campbell   He said, 'I just want to report it as a normal crime.'

Finally, some sense was breaking through. It was like coming up for air.

Other witnesses also failed to provide the damning profile of me that the prosecution wanted to create. Former Assistant Commissioner Ian Johnston, once my boss in the Met, was now the chief constable of the British Transport Police, and his opinion of my conduct would carry a lot of weight. He had been called by the prosecution to confirm that I had lied about the location of my car, and that the false location I had given had caused him to launch a major investigation. Which was why we were delighted to hear him say under examination by Horwell that, while I had lied, I was competent and able as an officer. Chief Constable Johnston seemed to me to be the perfect character referee: he was friendly and easy-going, despite being one of the country's most senior officers. When it was Mansfield's turn, he could use this character reference to start to build our case.

Johnston and Mansfield had history. Mansfield had savaged him during the Lawrence Inquiry, and Johnston had been battered by having to face the press with the Met's reaction to the report afterwards. He could have been hostile – but he was quite the opposite.

Part of the prosecution's case for misconduct was that I had complained about my treatment to *Time Out*, a weekly London magazine.

Mansfield   If Ali Dizaei had wanted to make a real fuss about the damage to his car, in your experience, could he have done more than go to *Time Out*?

Johnston   Oh yes. That man has a lot of connections with the press!

Mansfield   So if he wanted to boast about being a victim, he wouldn't go to *Time Out*. Isn't it right that you gave him permission to speak to any members of the press?

Johnston   Yes. As vice-chairman of the National Black Police Association, he can say or do whatever he likes with the press.

Mansfield   Do you think there was a conflict between his role of legal advisor to the NBPA and being a superintendent?

Johnston   Yes. It's a very difficult position to be in.

Mansfield   Do you remember Mr Otter putting a position paper to you about that conflict?

Johnston   Absolutely. I had to advise both of them. There were major tensions between these two individuals.

Mansfield (innocently)   Oh? What tension was that?

Johnston   They were not getting on. I had to arbitrate over a number of matters relating to NBPA work and his role as a superintendent in the Met.

Which, if we had scripted it, could not have made the foundations of our case that Chief Supt Otter had made my working life almost impossible in a more convincing way. Then, there was the consequence of my lie. Mansfield pointed out that three black officers, all NBPA members, had suffered car damage on the same day.

Mansfield   That dictated how you would deal with this incident?

Johnston   Yes.

Mansfield   Whether Mr Dizaei was parked in Selfridges' car park or here, it would have made no difference, would it?

Johnston   No.

Deputy Assistant Commissioner John Grieve, now Professor Emeritus at London Metropolitan University, was called for the same reason, but under cross-examination, Mansfield had him confirm that there was racism in the police force, and some new information: a fourth black police officer based at Notting Hill had been attacked on the same day. Four black officers, we now knew, had been the victims of crime in the same area on the same day.

Mansfield   So the scale of the subsequent investigation had nothing to do with Mr Dizaei?

Grieve   No.

Mansfield   Would the location of the car have made any difference?

Grieve   Not really.

There was still a mountain of damaging evidence, and we could not escape the central problem: I had not told the truth when asked. The witness who could effectively send me straight to jail was my boss at the station, Chief Superintendent Otter.

Chief Supt Otter was a convincing witness for the prosecution. He was smart, good-looking and well-spoken. The son of a clergyman, he was at his best when speaking in public, and had the gift of being able to win an audience over to his point of view. He normally came across as honest and very sincere. But the stakes were high here and he too had his reputation on the line. I was so concerned that I had even prepared a short briefing on him for Mansfield, where I warned him of Chief Supt Otter's ability. We might have had a bad relationship that brought out the worst in both of us, but he must have impressed the jury in the fifteen minutes during which the prosecution examined him.

During the two and a half days of cross-examination, a longer session than any other witness, Mansfield made him look less sympathetic. Early in his cross-examination, Mansfield wanted Chief Supt Otter to admit that I was disliked. Chief Supt Otter, diplomatically, preferred to say I was 'controversial'.

Mansfield   So you don't remember writing a memo or a paper saying that your colleagues all hated Dizaei, but the level of distaste depended on who you spoke to?

I held my breath. I realised immediately that this was a direct quote from a letter written to Chief Supt Norman as part of the Helios investigation – a letter which, for the purpose of the trial, effectively didn't exist. Chief Supt Otter knew that there was an agreement not to mention Helios in court. Did Mansfield know what he was doing?

Otter Absolutely not.

Mansfield Are you sure?

Otter I am absolutely sure I have never written anything like that.

Once more, Mansfield asked Chief Supt Otter to confirm that he was sure. After all, he pointed out, being in the witness box in the Old Bailey was stressful, and he might have forgotten. Otter confirmed, relying on the understanding that Helios material would not be mentioned, he was certain he was telling the truth. Mansfield paused, and produced the letter that Chief Supt Otter had written to Chief Supt Norman.

Mansfield (passing the letter to Otter) Can you read the bottom paragraph to the jury, please?

Otter 'Colleagues all hate him; the level of hatred depends on who you speak to...'

Mansfield Thank you very much! You don't need to read the rest!

It was a high-risk stunt, but it worked. I thought it was a stroke of genius from Mansfield. Chief Supt Otter had his credibility wrecked by a letter he never thought would come into the courtroom. Mansfield didn't let up, painting a picture – an accurate picture – of the way that Chief Supt Otter had left me exposed and had not supported me as his member of staff. Mansfield pointed out that soon after I joined the station at Notting Hill, I was asked by Chief Supt Otter to create a diversity report which identified the white officers who stopped a disproportionate number of black suspects to search them. 'Did you think of the repercussions for him?' Mansfield asked. Chief Supt Otter admitted he didn't.

'Should you not have cared if your deputy was exposed to the risk of being marginalised as a result of your instructions?' He had to admit, yes he should. Mansfield produced my application for Extended Interviews, which – pre-Helios – Chief Supt Otter had supported enthusiastically, and my application for promotion to chief superintendent, made only a few weeks later, but after Helios had begun. Chief Supt Otter had given me a poor reference. In his cross-examination, Mansfield compared the two documents, picking at the criticisms Chief Supt Otter had made of me.

Mansfield   You said that Mr Dizaei does not evidence his examples.

Otter   Which bit?

Mansfield   He said he was commended by the home secretary, but you say he didn't provide evidence of this. Is that right?

Otter   Yes.

Mansfield (withering)   But Mr Otter, *you were in the audience when he received the commendation!*

I was surprised by the jury's reaction. Some were grinning with disbelief and two were shaking their heads. The prosecution's key witness had crumbled. Horwell called Chief Supt Otter back into the box for re-examination, but he was unable to repair the damage Mansfield had caused. I had known Chief Supt Otter since we were sergeants, but I had never seen him shaken before.

The course provided by Avon and Somerset had not worked as well as he thought it would.

One hour later, the other prosecution witness who arguably finished up damaging the case against me, rather than adding to it, was former Sergeant Ian Kibblewhite. He had since been promoted to inspector, but I remembered him as a troublemaker, stirring up complaints, when he was Chief Supt Otter's staff officer. Unknown to Inspector Kibblewhite, he had already been mentioned in Chief Supt Otter's testimony, in reply to a question from Mansfield.

Again, Horwell's examination was brief and to the point. I had told Sgt Kibblewhite the car was parked near the police station, he confirmed. It was now Mansfield's turn: he concentrated on the controversy about why I was allowed to park in the station yard. He wanted to show how I had become disliked among the junior ranks.

Mansfield   How many people complained about Mr Dizaei's car?

Kibblewhite Well over fifty.

Mansfield   You used to encourage these complaints, didn't you?

Kibblewhite I didn't think it was right for anyone to park in the back yard. There isn't enough room.

Mansfield   Did you know that your boss, Chief Superintendent Otter, had given Mr Dizaei permission to park there?

Kibblewhite No, I didn't.

Mansfield   Basically, you were mischief-making, without knowing that your boss had given permission for Mr Dizaei to park there.

Kibblewhite No, I didn't know he had been given permission.

Having set Inspector Kibblewhite up as a troublemaker, Mansfield got to his point. He produced the article from the *Guardian* in which I had complained that discrimination in the police service was a form of 'ethnic cleansing'. Kibblewhite had objected to the article at the time.

Mansfield   Have you seen this article?

Kibblewhite Yes, I have read it.

Mansfield   What do you think of it?

Kibblewhite It annoyed a lot of people.

Mansfield (irritated)   I don't care about a lot of people. I want to know whether it annoyed you.

Kibblewhite They were not good words to use.

Mansfield   Why not?

Kibblewhite I didn't like the words 'ethnic cleansing' because of Kosovo.

Mansfield   Do you think there is discrimination against black staff in the police force?

Kibblewhite It's not up to me.

Mansfield (irritated again) You have a view, don't you? Why
              don't you share it with the jury?

Kibblewhite I think there is discrimination, but it's not as bad as
              it's…

Mansfield (holding up the newspaper article) Do you remember
              this article in the *Guardian*?

Kibblewhite I read the *Daily Mail*.

Mansfield Did you stick this article on the wall and conduct
              more mischief?

Kibblewhite I never did that.

One hour previously, Chief Supt Otter had confirmed that he
had reprimanded Inspector Kibblewhite for pinning the article
up, decorated with abusive remarks. If we had wanted a witness
to show the damage that canteen culture can do in the force, we
couldn't have chosen one better than Inspector Kibblewhite. It
was our good fortune that the prosecution chose him for us.

It was also our good fortune that the prosecuting advocates
seemed to think it would be so easy to convict me that they
sometimes seemed over-confident. Which brings us to the strange
case of Detective Sergeant 'Susan Collins' and her surveillance
evidence. We don't know her real name – as with all surveillance
officers, the name used for her is a pseudonym.

With the prosecution able to introduce the fact that I was under
surveillance, the surveillance logs could be used as evidence, and
the officers who compiled the logs were important witnesses. It
was vital for the prosecution to establish that the car was in
Emperor's Gate, not Cole Place, as I had (untruthfully) claimed.

It was also important for the surveillance officers to confirm that I had noted the damage sometime after 4 pm, not 1.15 pm.

For this, they were to use the surveillance logs compiled by 'Susan Collins' and her superior, 'Eddie Evans'.

A surveillance log isn't written by the surveillance officer. It is dictated into a microphone, and transcribed by a loggist, who might be miles away from the scene, and simply writes down, word-for-word, what is being said. This means that the undercover officer doesn't attract attention, and that the log is an accurate record of what is happening. It is contemporaneous: nothing is added later, or embellished using hindsight. That is why a surveillance log has such great value as evidence.

The 'Susan Collins' log wasn't contemporaneous. At least, one version of it was not. Three different surveillance logs offered detailed information about what I had been doing on 6 September 2000 at 4.15 pm. The contemporaneous one offers this version: 'Dizaei goes into his car. He is carrying folders, correspondence, and he sits in his car. He is talking on the mobile phone. He drives off.'

It's not an unusual log entry. A good surveillance officer reports exactly what is happening, no matter how dull it seems, as it may be important in the future. There were files full of logs showing me climbing into cars and getting out of them, entering buildings and leaving them, standing up and sitting down. Most of these entries, however, were not important, as this one was to become.

Later on 6 September, 'Susan Collins' added a footnote to the log. It stated that I had walked round my car, and touched it. The new entry was countersigned by 'Eddie Evans'. A later version of this log incorporates my alleged walk around my car, and has me touching the paintwork, as if the note had been made at the time. 'Collins' had produced one version to her sergeant, another to another officer, and the senior investigating officer had found there was a discrepancy. As the court was later told she was subject to misconduct proceedings.

It also emerged that she had kept a hand-written log. The third log had no mention of the walk-and-touch routine. This information dribbled out over a period of two months. Not only were the logs different in the detail of what I did, but they seemed to suggest that she was in two different locations, and 'Eddie Evans' was both with her and not with her.

The truth: I didn't walk round the car and touch it. I knew already that it was damaged, so I drove to the station and then reported it. When the surveillance officers saw the response to my reporting it, when roads were shut and my car was dusted for prints based on scratches that they didn't know had been added to it, they must have wondered what they had missed.

'Evans' was called as the prosecution witness, although it wasn't his log. He was a strong witness under Horwell's friendly questioning which skirted, but didn't confront, the problems of the non-contemporaneous log.

Mansfield	Do you consider yourself a good surveillance officer?
Evans	Yes, I do.
Mansfield	Is your log produced contemporaneously?
Evans	Yes.
Mansfield	And is it important that you pay attention to detail?
Evans	Yes.
Mansfield	You are to be congratulated. You have paid attention to detail, Mr Evans. At seven minutes past four, you say that Mr Dizaei came up to his car, and he had a phone in his hand, and he is also carrying correspondence. That's a lot of good detail.

Evans   It's what we are trained for.

Mansfield asked Evans to explain what happened next. Evans told the jury that I had walked round the car, and appeared to touch the bodywork.

Mansfield   I see. Where is that in the log?

Evans   It's not in the log.

Mansfield (feigning surprise)   Oh, why not?

Evans   It's added at the bottom.

Mansfield studied the extra note on the log, as if he was reading it for the first time, noting that in the addendum I had walked round the car about five times and had touched the car.

Mansfield   Did he touch the car?

Evans   He appeared to touch the car.

Mansfield   It says here that he touched the car. Now you tell the jury he only appeared to touch the car. Which one is it?

Evans   He went like this… *(making a touching motion with his hand)*

Mansfield   Oh, I see. He went like this *(mimicking with his hand)*. Did he touch the car, or only appear to touch the car?

Evans   He touched the car.

Once more, Mansfield made 'Evans' confirm that I had touched the car, not appeared to touch it. Once more, 'Evans' confirmed that yes, I had touched the car.

Mansfield   Why did you not put that observation in your log as it was happening?

Evans   It wasn't important.

Mansfield (sarcastic)   But it was important that he was carrying correspondence?

The courtroom was tense as 'Evans' confirmed his location on a large map – about 150 yards from me and my car. Mansfield added, archly, that he must have excellent eyesight to see all this detail.

Mansfield   Final point, Mr Evans, how many hands does Mr Dizaei have?

Evans (perplexed)   Two.

Mansfield   Well, let's think about that. You say he is on the phone talking to someone, and he has correspondence under his other arm. So tell me, *how exactly did he touch the car?*

3 **For the defence**

The prosecution had rested their case. I was scared. I was going into the witness box as a witness in my own defence. If I did a poor job, if I was unclear, if the jury didn't like me, if the prosecution tied me in knots or revealed a damning piece of evidence, I couldn't blame anyone else but myself.

The courtroom was packed with officers from Operation Helios, listening to my examination at the hands of Michael Mansfield. That, of course, was to be the easy part. Horwell had not been at his best when presenting the case for the prosecution, but he still knew how to rile me. For the first three hours, I was getting increasingly anxious. I was fighting him, snapping at him, sounding like a man with something to hide. I had to find some serenity.

The details of my aggressive telephone messages to Mandy, the intimate details of my private life, my marriage and every flaw in my personality were all going to be paraded and mocked in front of the people I considered my enemies. It was humiliating, and hard to bear.

It helped to be able to confess my fault, without shame. We had prepared for this. Horwell held up a paper on which were printed the values and principles expected of a Metropolitan Police officer. 'Honesty and integrity!' he chided me, asking if I met those standards when I lied about my car.

I didn't, I admitted. 'Sometimes I fall short. But I learn and try to do better…I am a human being with the same frailties and weaknesses as anybody else.' It was the truth. I hoped that the jury would find some forgiveness.

Horwell didn't think they would. Time and again he found different words to ask me whether I had lied. Time and again, I admitted to him that I had, and time and again I told him that it was because of the treatment I was getting at Kensington police station. I told the truth: I was extremely sorry, and had been ever since I opened my mouth on 6 September 2000.

It was a relief to get out of the witness box after two days, and let someone else do the talking on my behalf.

Assistant Commissioner Tariq Ghaffur was a reluctant witness on my behalf. Understandably he wasn't keen to testify, but his evidence was vital in my case. He didn't want to appear as a defence witness, because it would be hard for him to admit in court that he had warned me about his fellow officers. But it was vital evidence to keep me out of prison. We decided to subpoena him: his evidence was that important.

Three years previously, when I had shown AC Ghaffur the two application forms on which Chief Supt Otter had written comments, the positive ones on my application for EI, the negative on my application for promotion, he had attached the sticky note to the second application form, and written on it, 'Smacks of personal vendetta'. I still had the note, and was determined to use it. When my legal team told him that they would subpoena him, he relented, and appeared voluntarily to tell the court that I had been treated unfairly. When Horwell started his cross-examination, you could see why AC Ghaffur didn't want to appear in the witness box, because the only way for the prosecution to taint the power of his evidence was to question his professional judgement. Although AC Ghaffur was one of the most respected officers in the Metropolitan Police, Horwell decided to try and question his professional ability. That was a mistake.

Horwell	You're not really experienced enough to assess an application, are you?
Ghaffur	I have been a police officer for twenty-eight years, served in several police forces and my competence has never been an issue. Of course I can assess an application for chief superintendent.

Four times, Horwell brought him back to the question of the sticky note, presumably hoping that AC Ghaffur might say it was an error of judgement on his part. Four times, Ghaffur told the jury that he thought there was a vendetta against me. Once again, Horwell had accidentally helped to make my case. The contents of the notes were ingrained in the jury's minds. The prosecution was amplifying our case, and Horwell had done it by trying to ridicule one of the most senior officers at Scotland Yard. But I wasn't complaining. The jury seemed equally baffled as to why the most senior and Asian police officer in UK was having his integrity and professional competence questioned.

After Ghaffur had left the witness box, Mansfield called Dr Elham Hashemi. Privately Ellie must have regretted the day she met me, and by this time she was no friend of the police force. She had launched a formal complaint against the Helios officers, because of the way she was treated by the officers investigating me. I asked her to come to court to give evidence that I had called her at around 1.40, when I had discovered the damage to my car.

She confirmed to the jury that I had rung her as soon as I had discovered the damage. I spoke to her for twenty-five minutes, griping about the inconvenience, she remembered. Usually, we didn't speak for anything like that length of time.

Horwell asked to introduce a phone transcript of the conversation Ellie and I once had about her borrowing my car.

To recap: she had fully comprehensive insurance. Naturally cautious, she asked me to add her as a named driver to my insurance for one week. I told her that whatever happened, she was not to use the car for work since my policy did not allow that. She said, 'Yeah.'

From this evidence, Horwell wanted to make the case that I was conspiring with her to defraud the insurance company and therefore she could not be believed. They decided that I was hinting to her that if she had an accident while using the car for work, she was to lie to the police. The allegation had – not surprisingly – been rejected by the Crown Prosecution Service as the basis for a charge of fraud, because it was plainly rubbish. It relied on putting a meaning on our conversation that was the exact opposite of the words that were spoken, and using only one out of three separate translations of the conversation. Also, Ellie hadn't had an accident, or made a claim, so no fraud could have been committed. All she had done was to drive a fully insured car and to say 'Yeah'.

Not only was this accusation rubbish, but the transcript existed only because of Operation Helios: another reason why the conversation should never have been part of my trial. Horwell now asked the judge for permission to refer to the conversation in court. The judge agreed; Mansfield objected, without success. Horwell's strategy seemed to be to suggest that Ellie was capable of lying, just as we had sought to show up Chief Supt Otter and Inspector Kibblewhite. If she could plot with me against a car insurance company, she would certainly fib about the time and duration of a telephone call.

Back in Court Seven, Horwell suggested to Ellie that she didn't take a call from me at 1.40 pm, and I hadn't told her about the car. She disagreed, telling the jury she remembered the time because she was on her lunch break at the university. Horwell didn't seem to know exactly what Ellie did for a living or what our relationship was. If he did, he didn't seem to understand.

Horwell   And how does it look to your students that you
            spoke for twenty-five minutes on the phone?

Hashemi   I am a senior research fellow in academia. We're not
            the army or the police. I can do what I like in my
            office. I can speak to who I like when I am there, I
            can sleep there if I wish. I am an academic, what do
            you mean, 'What impression did it make?'? What
            are you talking about?

Horwell (quickly moving on)   Was there a relationship between
            the two of you?

Hashemi   Yes. But we didn't have a sexual relationship if that's
            what you mean. I am a Muslim.

Horwell   Why did you not tell the police that Mr Dizaei called
            you at 1.40 pm?

Hashemi (annoyed)   I was never asked!

Horwell then introduced the transcript, translated from
Farsi, of our conversation about car insurance. This must have
seemed odd to the jury, who were under the impression that
Ellie was there to establish the time of a completely different
phone call that happened months afterwards. He suggested
that, according to the transcript, Ellie might have been trying
to defraud the insurance company. Ellie countered that she
wasn't because she was fully insured. Horwell persisted; Ellie
stuck to her answer:

Hashemi   What difference does it make? There was no
            accident, no claim, whether I used it for work or
            not made no difference. My own policy allows me

	to drive any motor vehicle on the road for whatever reason.
Horwell	He says, 'So if anything happens, you were not going to work', and you say, 'Yeah'.
Hashemi	So? How many times have you been on the phone when someone is talking, and said 'yeah'?

Horwell asked again why Ellie had not offered this explanation to the police. Ellie countered again that the police had never asked for an explanation.

Horwell	But they did come to see you, Dr Hashemi.
Hashemi	That was because I had made a formal complaint against them.

After eight weeks in Court Seven, my trial was suddenly on the point of collapse. Ellie was about to mention Operation Helios, the CIB3 surveillance, or her problems with Norman and the investigating officers. As Helios was excluded from the evidence, this would probably lead to a mistrial. In private conference with the judge and the barristers present, Mansfield pointed this out and suggested that Horwell choose another line of questioning. The judge agreed, telling Horwell that this wasn't why Ellie was called as a witness.

When we resumed, Horwell gave his cross-examination a last shot.

Horwell	I suggest to you that Mr Dizaei did not call you. This telephone call didn't happen.
Hashemi	Are you calling me a liar?

The courtroom was silent. No one moved. I may never have been a practising barrister, but I remembered the advice of my tutors: avoid calling a witness a liar at all costs; suggest they are lying, and use evidence to back your suggestion, but don't accuse a witness of lying under oath unless you are very sure of yourself. In layman's terms: when you are in a hole, stop digging. Ellie, now furious, repeated her question.

Hashemi   *Are you calling me a liar?*

Horwell   Yes. I am.

Hashemi *(addressing judge)* Your lordship, I want to say something.

Judge Hyam Go on.

Hashemi   I am not sure what I am doing here. I have been asked to give evidence about some stupid crime about a scratched car that I don't even understand. The amount of humiliation I have had to endure coming here is reprehensible. There are officers sitting here who have listened to my intimate telephone conversations and have probably had a little giggle as they were listening to me speaking to Mr Dizaei. I had to endure all that and I have come here because I believe in telling the truth. You might think it is acceptable to come here and lie, but this is the first time in my life that I have sworn on the Holy Koran. In my religion, you don't do that very often. I have had to endure this humiliation, and if you honestly think I have broken my principles and sworn on the Koran to

come here to lie about some scratched car, you are
badly mistaken.

Barristers are taught to look for the reaction of the jurors if they
want to know how successful their cross-examination has been.
As Ellie finished, one of the members of the jury punched the air.
You could confidently say this was a bad sign for the prosecution.
Horwell tried to retain his composure, and ploughed on. In
layman's terms, he kept digging, using one last desperate tactic to
try to discredit Ellie:

Horwell   And has anybody prepared you for that statement?

Hashemi   What do you mean?

Horwell   Have Mr Dizaei's lawyers prepared you for that
               speech?

Hashemi   The only thing that Mr Dizaei's lawyers told me to
               expect from today was to be humiliated, which I
               have been.

And with that, Horwell finally accepted that he had no more
questions for this witness.

Mansfield coaxed me back into the witness box one more time
to give evidence about this telephone call. Horwell suggested
the insurance fraud story to me again. I asked him to read the
part of the transcript where I had told her to lie to the insurance
company. He couldn't, because there wasn't one.

'But that's what you intended, Mr Dizaei,' he told me, not
letting up.

'You want to draw inferences,' I said. 'The fact is: they are not
there.'

The Crown Prosecution Service guidelines are strict on when

a Treasury Counsel should be employed. 'Treasury Counsel are a scarce and valuable resource. In general they should only be instructed if a case displays points of substantial public interest, or presents evidential/procedural difficulties.' My scratched car had now occupied almost eight weeks of court time and had surprisingly tested the competence of the First Treasury Counsel.

At the end of a trial, there are three long speeches. First, the prosecution sums up its case. Second, the defence provides its own summation. Finally, the judge sums up the case and offers the jury guidelines as to what facts are important to consider. After weeks of testimony, these summations can have a make-or-break effect on a trial.

Horwell went first. His summation was different from his opening address, in which he portrayed me as a self-seeking publicist. His witnesses, especially AC Johnston, had not supported that argument. Instead, he concentrated on the fact that I had lied, as everyone, myself included, now agreed.

Mansfield had to counter this by asking the jury to look at a bigger picture. 'I wonder if any of you have seen those drawings where you put your head very close, and all you see is dots...but you take a few steps back and you begin to see the real picture...' he began. Speaking without notes, he commiserated with them that they had been stuck in the Old Bailey for many weeks over a scratched car. 'Ask yourself,' he said, being careful not to mention Operation Helios by name, but stretching to the very limit of what he was allowed to say to portray the case against me as the result of official paranoia, 'why was Ali Dizaei under surveillance? Why did they tap his phone? Who considered this necessary? Think about that when you retire.'

Mansfield has often been criticised as a showman: speaking without notes for two and a half hours, he didn't so much sum up the case against me as make fun of it. He mimicked Evans again, waggling his hand in the way I was supposed to have done when I made my fictitious walk around my car and touched the paintwork with both hands full. The jury began to laugh at this point and I could see that the judge was getting irritated. But Mansfield was only doing his job. He sarcastically questioned his own memory. Maybe the prosecution had mentioned my desire to seek publicity in *Time Out* magazine in its closing statement, he said, and he had just missed it. Or maybe, he pointed out, Horwell chose not to mention it.

He called AC Ghaffur's cross-examination by Horwell 'extraordinary'. He told a story of a police force that tolerated rogue officers who would do anything to convict me of a crime, because I was not one of them.

He reminded the jury of Inspector Kibblewhite, who was, he suggested, an example of the kind of colleagues I had to work with.

Halfway through Mansfield's performance, Horwell abruptly got up and stalked out of the courtroom. And so Horwell wasn't there to see Mansfield sorrowful at the calibre of the police witnesses that the prosecution had called.

Nor did Horwell hear Mansfield ask why the other incidents of damage on the same day, also against black police officers, were not investigated with roadblocks and forensic teams.

No one enjoys standing trial. I was still worried, humiliated and angry. But listening to Mansfield, I could believe in myself and for the first time could allow myself to hope that I would not go to prison. Squeezed into the wooden benches of the tiny public gallery, almost directly above Horwell's vacant seat, were around thirty of my colleagues from the NBPA. As we left court that day, we stupidly hugged each other as if I had won.

'For God's sake,' Egan said, appalled, 'get a hold of yourselves.' He was right: the judge hadn't spoken yet. As the senior figure in the courtroom, and the last person to speak to the jury before they retired to consider their verdict, his comments would carry the most weight. If he thought Mansfield had been too flippant, he might try to redress the balance, by pointing out the strength of the prosecution evidence.

The Helios team were relying on this, and were still confident. Norman was so confident that he had popped off to Alicante to play golf two days before the summing up. Before he left, he had time to brief the journalists who were covering the trial, telling those who agreed to sign confidentiality agreements that whatever happened, I would never wear the uniform again, as I didn't have the integrity to be a police officer. When he said this, I was still, technically, an innocent man. I hadn't even been found guilty of an internal disciplinary offence.*

Judge Hyam took a full day to sum up the case. Just before lunch he wondered aloud if there was anything he should have mentioned but had forgotten. I was hopping up and down in my seat, because he had not mentioned the multiple surveillance logs. I pleaded with Mansfield to mention it, which he did. The judge said that he was most grateful, and went on to distil the case into some simple questions for the jury.

The first: was my car ever in Cope Place? It was a fair question.

His second point was a major advantage for me. 'The two allegations stand or fall together,' he said. My mouth hung open. Mansfield and Egan were too experienced to portray their surprise, but they were shocked.

I had been indicted on two different, and distinct, charges. The first was for perverting the course of justice, alleging that I was trying to manipulate the investigation into my scratched car. The second was for misconduct in public office, because I lied about where it was when it was scratched. I could have been found not guilty of perverting the course of justice, but still guilty of misconduct. It would not have been as severe a penalty, but would still have finished my career.

* Again, this is covered in the report of the Morris Inquiry, 10.61–
  10.63

By saying that the two allegations were effectively one, the judge was asking the jury to consider whether they believed the car could have been in Cope Place when it was damaged. It was an all-or-nothing verdict, but one which had a much better chance of going in my favour. We were delighted.

While the jury is out, there is literally nothing to do. You can't go anywhere or do anything. I couldn't sleep that night, pacing the floor, reliving the vindications and the humiliations of the last month. The next morning, I was back at the Old Bailey canteen in my usual spot, wondering who the new detective chief inspector was who had joined the prosecution team. She wasn't part of the CIB3 team, and I didn't know her.

I found out from a colleague that she had a very special job: if I was found guilty, she had my dismissal notice signed and ready to issue, in person, on the spot. It was a modern version of the summary justice of the Newgate courthouse.

The jury debated in secret for ninety minutes, and then decided on lunch. I went across the road for a sandwich and sat with a journalist from the BBC *Newsnight* team who had been following my case; she kindly paid for my bagel, which I couldn't eat. The advice from people who were more experienced in this than me was not to hold my breath waiting for a verdict – with the amount of evidence to consider, it might be four days before they decided. I would have to eat sometime soon.

At 2.15, I wandered back from lunch to find an agitated court usher looking for me. We had a verdict, she said. Everyone was taken by surprise. From various parts of London, the entire cast were rushing back to the Old Bailey. Mansfield had to bolt down what he thought would be a leisurely lunch at a restaurant to which he had taken the solicitors who worked on my defence. My colleagues in the NBPA who had supported me would not make it back in time – they were at work. Only my friend DC Fitzroy Theodore and Sadiq Khan, my employment lawyer, managed to get back to court to hear the verdict. Instead, the many police who worked in the building packed the gallery to see what would happen to one of their own.

I was about to go into court, and an Asian officer pressed a small square of material into my hand. 'It is from the house of God in Mecca,' he said. 'Hold it in your hand when you go in.' I sat in Court Seven, shaking, gripping the cloth.

At 2.30 pm on 11 April 2003, the jury filed into their seats for the last time. To my eyes, they looked grim and tight lipped. That meant they thought I was guilty. The foreman had often looked at me during the trial, but now he avoided meeting my eyes. I stared at my feet instead, seconds away from being broken.

I had to stand for the verdict; my legs were as shaky as the rest of me. I felt sick.

'Members of the jury, have you reached a verdict?'

'We have,' said the foreman.

'On the charge of perverting the course of justice, do you find the defendant guilty or not guilty?'

'Not guilty.'

'On the charge of misconduct in public office, do you find the defendant guilty or not guilty?'

'Not guilty.'

I punched the air. 'God bless you,' I said to the jury. I sobbed as I hugged Mansfield, wetting his gown with my tears. The nightmare was finally over.

Except that, as the prosecution was about to point out to the judge, it wasn't.

4 **Not so fast**

The jury, by making its decision so quickly, had given the Met a problem.

It was ten years to the day since the murder of Stephen Lawrence. If the court case was over, the press would not be shy in making the connection between the murder that had uncovered institutional racism in the police and the runaway train that was Operation Helios – an investigation that I was now free to talk about. There were around thirty reporters who had scrambled to the Old Bailey for the verdict. Television news teams waited outside. Peter Bottomley MP, who had been so supportive, was there as well.

As I sobbed all over Mansfield's gown, Horwell was already clearing his throat to alert Judge Hyam: M'lord would be aware, he pointed out, that there were still nine more counts of false accounting on the indictment, and could the Crown please have ten days to decide whether it wanted to proceed with them? During that time, could we keep reporting restrictions in place?

The nine counts related to eight separate discrepancies in my mileage claims, a total of £455 that the Met said I had claimed when I wasn't entitled to. It was, after three and a half years and a trial, all that was left. Were they really contemplating a prosecution for fiddling expenses – or, as the Met's press officers grandly briefed reporters, 'false accounting'?

As they had had quite long enough to bring the prosecution to court, none of us expected it to go ahead. We were annoyed, but I was elated at the jury's verdict, and I didn't think for a second that I would ever be back in court. We thought they had asked for ten days to let the press lose interest, to move on to the next story.

Around thirty of us crowded into a nearby coffee shop. I called my mother in Iran to tell her the verdict as the TV cameras pointed in my face. I wasn't free, it wasn't over, but for the first time I had some idea of how it might feel when it was.

Nine days later, I'm sitting in a coffee shop in Maidenhead. The NBPA has a press conference planned for the next day in a hotel opposite New Scotland Yard, and I am relishing the opportunity to finally have my say. My phone rings. It's Ian Lewis, my solicitor at Rowe Cohen.

'You won't believe this, Ali,' he said, 'they decided to go for it on the mileage.'

At the Old Bailey the next day, a place I never wanted to see again, it was getting personal. We're back in the canteen: at one end, Mansfield, Egan, myself, my solicitors, Ravi and Leroy from the NBPA. At the other, the prosecution. I was finding new depths to my misery, and looking at them, thinking about what they had taken from me, for the first time I lost it. I wanted to march over to them and have it out right there.

'You bastards,' I shouted, getting up. Ravi and Leroy, wisely, pulled me back, or I'd have been facing more than a charge of false accounting. We made it into court without me being tempted to dispense a more direct form of justice, to hear that I would be bailed until October – six more months of torment. We also heard that Horwell would no longer be prosecuting. His cross-examination skills were needed elsewhere. The Senior Treasury Counsel only did scratched cars; his junior devil, Crispin Aylett, took care of prosecutions based on mileage expenses.

The prosecution didn't allege that I had invented journeys,

merely that I hadn't taken the most direct route, or inflated the mileage. So instead of going directly from my house to the M4 motorway during the rush hour, I had taken a longer journey through back roads I knew, a route that was longer but more reliable. When I claimed a trip from London to Bristol, I had entered a mileage that was longer than the distance to the centre of Bristol: or, as the prosecution assumed in reviewing my expense claims, the distance to a mosque in the centre of Bristol. Egan, who always took the prosecution case seriously, pointed this out, much to my irritation.

That's because I wasn't going to Bristol city centre, and I didn't visit other places to go to a mosque any more than my colleagues took business trips to London to pop in to Westminster Abbey. As was perfectly obvious, I was going to a meeting at the headquarters of Somerset and Avon police force, which was a longer journey. The claim was correct, the form wasn't.

So the process of sifting the evidence started again. In the offices of Rowe Cohen in Manchester, there was a room that had long since been closed off to normal business: it was the Helios room, stuffed with files related to my case, and in that room a junior solicitor called Imran Khan was tasked with finding the evidence. Meanwhile, at a cost of more than forty times the sum that I was supposed to have fiddled, we had to employ an expert to drive every journey mentioned in the indictments. As he meandered through the back roads of Henley, Imran compared my expense claims with the Helios surveillance logs.

The evidence presented in my first trial had detailed my movements over many months: conferences visited, meetings attended, journeys on NBPA business. My paranoia had paid off, because I had been so cautious in claiming expenses that there were many journeys I hadn't claimed for. Using the prosecution's own evidence, I didn't owe the Met £455, the Met owed me more than £4,000. I couldn't wait to get to court and see Mansfield make a case based on Imran's evidence.

As my court appointment approached, my colleague Clive Morris, at the NBPA, received a call from a journalist. 'I hear they are going to drop the case against Ali Dizaei,' the journalist said, asking for comment. It was the first any of us had heard of it. I called Ian Lewis: he didn't know anything either, but he promised to call the Crown Prosecutor to fish for information, using his considerable ability to do exactly that.

'Are you dropping the case?' he asked. There was silence on the other end of the phone.

'We can't tell you,' was the hesitant reply. That was a big hint. If they weren't thinking about dropping the case, then a simple 'No' would have been the answer.

On 9 September, I was in the Helios room in Manchester, going through expense claims with Imran Khan. He answered the phone, talked for a moment, hung up and smiled at me.

'It's been dropped,' he said. 'They want you in court on Friday.'

No, we said, we can make it on Monday. After all this time, we wanted to do things our way. We weren't going to rush.

On Sunday, the *Independent* leaked the news. 'That is expected to cause considerable embarrassment to the Metropolitan Police, which spent months gathering evidence,' it said. This guaranteed that on Monday, the press was ready to hear that the CPS was offering no evidence.

I walked out of the Old Bailey as a free man. I gave my one prepared line to the reporters who crowded me, making me feel like David Beckham. 'I feel absolutely relieved and delighted that I have been unequivocally acquitted of all the allegations that have been made,' I said, leaving the stage to Mansfield, who delighted in telling the waiting reporters that 'what has happened is of almost Orwellian proportions'.

As I walked to the NBPA press conference at the Club Quarters Hotel, I looked across at the hotel dining room, and there I saw the director of public prosecutions, the man responsible for dragging me through the courts and nearly sending me to prison, eating his lunch.

I was anxious to say that Helios should not be a reflection of the Metropolitan Police, but was more to do with the conduct of a handful of officers, who had seemed to be out of control and unaccountable; as a result it seemed to me they proceeded with an investigation long after it was obvious there was no criminal conduct to discover. Now we had to make sure that this could not happen again. That was the theme of the press conference: we could have been a lot tougher, more radical. I had every major news programme calling for interviews – we had already decided that I would only talk to those news outlets that would take the case seriously, not use it as a platform to rehash gossip and innuendo. If my accusers wanted to hide behind the cover of the Metropolitan Police, we were not going to give them that pleasure.

On Wednesday, I appeared on the *Today* programme, in the 8.10 slot usually reserved for senior politicians. Deputy Assistant Commissioner Stephen House, who I had never previously met, was the Met's representative. 'There are many of my colleagues who are in favour of equality and giving an excellent service to the people of London,' I said. 'I think you are talking about no more than a handful of individuals...All I want to be is a policeman, and to serve the people of London. The taxpayers demand I should go out and do some work.'

'It was only by having such a meticulous investigation that we got to the truth,' said DAC House, supporting my ambition to get back to the job, 'the last thing we want is a whispering campaign.'

As the two sides politely edged towards a reconciliation that was several years overdue, the Sunday tabloid press, aided by the 'handful of officers', had other ideas. There wasn't a whispering campaign, because they preferred to scream hysterically.

Six days after I thought I had been found not guilty, I had

been tried and convicted in the press. Mandy Darougeh had
been persuaded to sell her story: 'My hell as top cop's lover,' said
the headline in the *People*, '"Corruption cop" used police badge
to get free nightclub champagne' trumpeted the *Mail on Sunday*.
The *Daily Express* had named me the 'Casanova cop'.

Although I had patched up my relationship with Mandy,
who had since moved to Dubai, the reporters seemed to have
convinced her that I was claiming she was a stripper and a
prostitute, which of course wasn't true. Perhaps, having printed
that I was suspected of using drugs and being a spy in 2001, the
reporters were propping up a story that had failed to deliver the
knockout punch they were expecting.

Through my solicitors, I managed to sell my side of the story
to the *Mail on Sunday*, so that I had money available to clear my
name. A number of newspapers had claimed I was living beyond
my means – implying that I must have another source of income
– that I was a racist myself and that I had a large house in Henley,
rather than a police house.

While the media feasted on the details of the case that the
reporting restrictions had denied them for so long, there was still
an unresolved problem: what to do with me. I was suspended on
full pay, there were still outstanding internal disciplinary matters
against me, I had launched an employment tribunal case against
my employers, and everyone, me included, wanted the entire
problem to go away.

On 23 September, David Blunkett addressed the NBPA annual
conference in Cardiff, and told them that Commissioner Sir John
Stevens 'will take the steps necessary to ensure this matter is
closed down as soon as possible'. He admitted that he had been
brokering a solution 'behind the scenes'. He 'had witnessed events
in the last few days which he would not want repeated'.

'Behind the scenes' was actually a suite in the conference
hotel. Ravi Chand represented me. DAC House represented

the Met with a solicitor, alongside Catherine Crawford, clerk of the Metropolitan Police Authority, Sir Ronnie Flanagan, Her Majesty's Inspector of Police, and my representative from the Superintendents' Association. I wasn't sure what I wanted from the talks. The NBPA and my friends in the police wanted me to go back to work, to carry on where I had left off. I wanted that too. I had spent my life as a police officer and I still loved the job, even though I was beginning to forget what it was like to do it. My Iranian friends, and Natalie, had long since lost any confidence in the police, and urged me to take a pay-off: it would be calculated on how many years of service I would have lost and my probable finishing salary. The amount was estimated by my advisors to be between £1.5 million and £2 million. To do that, I would have to go back to work for one day, shake the hand of the commissioner to show there were no hard feelings, and resign the next day.

I couldn't do it. I wanted my job back. I was prepared to accept 'words of advice' on two of the outstanding disciplinary proceedings: my call to Mandy, and the way I dealt with the location of my car when it was scratched – a form of censure in which I would concede that I'd made mistakes – because that was fair. The Met would drop the remaining eight proceedings. That's the deal that was being brokered in a hotel suite as David Blunkett addressed the delegates downstairs.

Later, Ravi and I met Sir Ronnie at his flat in Pimlico, central London, to discuss the terms on which I could go back. Sir Ronnie was genuine and honest, and I liked him immediately. He was sympathetic, but he didn't have the power to make a deal. He would talk to the Met, he said.

At the last minute, when we thought we had a deal, it broke down. If I was going to return to work, the Met wanted me to work under the terms of a 'service confidence agreement'. I wouldn't be able to deal directly with members of the public. I wouldn't be able to manage staff. In my mind, I wouldn't be able to do any useful job. A service confidence agreement is used to rehabilitate officers who have been found to have committed serious breaches of police professional standards. It was totally out of proportion for anything I had done.

And so on 8 October, the NBPA told black Britons not to join the police. Ray Powell said, 'Our faith in the Met has collapsed'. From now on, it would not just boycott all the Met's activities to recruit officers from ethnic minorities, as it had announced after the case against me collapsed, it would actively campaign to stop the Met recruiting black officers.

The NBPA raised the stakes even further. There was also going to be a protest march on 17 November, but not just any march. One thousand black police officers would take the day off to march through central London, in uniform, to New Scotland Yard. This was, by any standards, a crisis. The home secretary called for more talks as 'a matter of urgency'. The mayor of London called the escalation 'dangerous'. The Met was 'extremely concerned'.

That's when the Home Office called on ACAS.

The Advisory Conciliation and Arbitration Service was founded in 1975 as a way for employees to resolve problems, but most of its notoriety comes from trying to resolve large-scale industrial disputes, such as the miners' strike of the 1980s. There was no precedent for it to get involved in a police staffing issue, but we were all desperate. With the help of the negotiators, we got a deal: no service confidence agreement. A return to work, my job back, disciplinary charges to be dropped, £60,000 in compensation and a promotion to chief superintendent three years after I earned it. I would finally get to go on the Senior Command Course. The NBPA would lift its boycott and postpone the march.

On 28 October 2003, I walked back into work for the first time since 18 January 2001. Sir John Stevens announced that I returned with my 'integrity demonstrably intact'. I had a new uniform – I had torn up my old one in anger years ago. I had a new job; and from the first moment I arrived back, I had the complete and unwavering support of the officers around me.

A couple of weeks later, I attended the AGM of the Metropolitan Black Police Association, in uniform. As I waited outside, I spotted the commissioner entering the building by a different route. He was going to address the meeting that morning to try and begin the process of rebuilding trust between the association and the Met. It would have been awkward for him to bump into me outside the mayor's office, in full view of the press.

Inside, he spoke to the delegates. Then, spotting me in the audience, he turned to me.

'Ali, I respect you for what you have done,' he said.

It was over.

Although it is never really over, because the problem we were trying to solve was only partly about my career, my mileage claims, and whether black police officers exercised their right to march through London. It was about whether the police forces of the United Kingdom can change for the better.

There was one more bump in my personal road back: twenty-four hours before the Police Complaints Authority was wound up on 31 March 2004, it tried to torpedo my deal. The Met had no right, it said, to offer to drop disciplinary proceedings. I had to face a misconduct hearing on nine charges.

Sir Alistair Graham, the chair of the PCA, was interviewed on BBC news on the evening of his departure. Black police officers should not get special treatment, he said. I could only wish him good riddance and hope that his successor, the chair of the Independent Police Complaints Commission, would overturn his decision. Thankfully, several months later, the IPCC did reverse the PCA's intervention. I received my words of advice about the way I spoke to Mandy. I accept that I made mistakes, and I have paid for them, and learned a lesson.

Even as the deal to reinstate me was being done, the bigger problem hit the headlines again when *The Secret Policeman*, a BBC documentary, was broadcast on 21 October 2003. Reporter Mark Daly went undercover as a police recruit and secretly taped the conversations of his fellow recruits.

'I'll stop him cos he's a Paki. Sad, innit, but I would. He's a Paki and I'm stopping him cos I'm fucking English,' says one.

'A dog born in a barn is still a dog. A Paki born in Britain is still a Paki,' says another.

PC Pulling said Stephen Lawrence's murderers should get 'diplomatic immunity', that Lawrence 'deserved it' and that the Macpherson report was a 'fucking kick in the bollocks for any white man'.

'They've done for this country what others should fucking do,' he said about Lawrence's murderers.*

The astonishing level of race hate that the nation saw could suggest that we're going backwards, but that would ignore the good work and commitment of the vast majority of police officers. The police force isn't perfect, but it's improving – and I want to help that.

On 19 February 2004, in a small room near the Home Office, Commissioner Stevens told racist police officers to 'get out of the Met now'. It was the first morning of an inquiry into professional standards in the Metropolitan Police chaired by Sir Bill Morris, the former general secretary of the Transport and General Workers' Union. 'Let me be unequivocal from the outset – there is no place in the Metropolitan Police for racists,' Sir John told the inquiry. 'If you do not believe in the fundamental right of all people to be treated with respect, dignity and compassion, then I do not want to share my service with you. You should not try to join. If you are

* You can find a full transcript of *The Secret Policeman* at http://www.blink.org.uk/docs/secret_policeman.htm. PC Pulling resigned from the North Wales Police soon after the programme was broadcast.

a serving police officer or staff member and cannot claim such a belief as your own, you should get out of the Met now.'

To be able to appear at the inquiry and give evidence in uniform felt like some vindication. To have the inquiry report call for 'a full independent case review' of what happened to me, because 'nothing less will do justice to those involved', was a good feeling. Another recommendation was that the Met doesn't comment on any officer's guilt or innocence until that is established in court. That would have made my life a lot easier.

I can't turn back the clock. What matters most is that there isn't another case like mine, ever. Sir Bill states in his report that he was 'left with the concern that there is no common understanding of diversity within [the Met] and that it is not embedded in the culture'. And while that is still the case, diversity, for police officers, is at its worst 'a source of fear and anxiety' and 'a serious issue of discrimination which must be tackled as a matter of priority'.

One of the reasons I wanted my job back is to help tackle those problems from the inside. The support I've had from my fellow officers – black and white – since I returned shows that we can, and we will – because in a multi-cultural country, there is simply no alternative.

Part five

Reconciliation

I didn't make the best impression when I walked into Bramshill Police College on 2 April 2004 for my first day on the Senior Command Course, three years, almost to the day, after I was first scheduled to be there. I was an hour late. Forty-five other chief superintendents from around the UK – the officers who had been selected to be the future leaders of the police service – were there on time. A few of them admitted to me afterwards that they thought the most likely reason for my lateness on the first day of my reintroduction to the police service was that I had been pulled off the course at the last minute, caught by a final unforeseen switchback in my three-year disciplinary process.

Actually, I was just plain late. I would have to buck up my ideas.

The Senior Command Course made me nervous. I was nervous because I had been out of operational policing for three years, a time in which the others on the course had been proving themselves as worthy of a place. I was nervous because I was notorious. I've always known that I haven't been popular among many members of the force outside London. I had plenty of evidence of that. If they had formed an opinion of me by reading the newspapers that had branded me the 'Casanova cop' and a troublemaker, I wasn't going to find many friends.

I was also suspicious. I was carrying a lot of mental baggage: it was hard for me to trust anyone, especially my fellow officers, because I had suffered at the hands of the police. I felt I had a point to prove, but I saw enemies everywhere. I had been given false hope so many times since 2001 that I was a part-time conspiracy theorist, second-guessing the intentions of the senior officers who had allowed me on the course.

The process had started three months earlier, when I discovered who would be running the course: former West Midlands Deputy Chief Constable Anne Summers was course director. For me, there couldn't have been a worse choice, or so I thought, as DCC Summers had been the independent police advisor who reviewed material from Helios, and provided guidance to the investigators. From six months into the investigation, it would have been regularly reviewed. The officers involved would have presented to her the results of their work on Helios, and she could have advised them to call a halt at any stage, telling them that the intrusion into my private life was unwarranted, or that the conduct of the investigation was disproportionate to the result. She didn't. On top of that, she had clearly signalled that she didn't like my conduct – for example, the way I spoke about women; but in fairness she had also asked Supt Norman to ensure that the investigators' personal views about my private life did not cloud their judgement.

The officer who reviewed and approved an investigation conceived to prove I was a criminal didn't seem like the ideal officer to evaluate my suitability as a senior officer. And although I didn't know her, I was wary of her for what I thought she had done to me. I travelled to Bramshill for a showdown meeting. I was accompanied by DAC Alan Brown, appointed to help me reintegrate into the Met. DAC Brown had immediately won my confidence with his honesty and support.

Despite my prejudice, I couldn't dislike DCC Summers either when I met her. She was professional, honest and direct. She was obviously sincere.

'We'll treat you fairly,' she promised. 'You will get a fair crack at this. Just you wait and see. And then when the course is over, you and I will sit down, and we'll talk it over.'

I was encouraged, but I wasn't convinced, and I still didn't know if it was worth even showing up. I still had the habit that I had picked up during the days of Helios of noting down what people said to me in case I needed it later, and I wrote down what she had said to me in the meeting. I liked DCC Summers, but I was still convinced that I might end up taking the police service to an employment tribunal if I felt I was unfairly treated on the course. If I did, her evaluation of me, and her prior opinion of me, were going to be part of my case. DAC Brown reassured me that I would get a fair chance, and I believed him.

Then my paranoia resurfaced when I heard the list of assessors on the course. Between April and October, we would be divided into five 'syndicates', teams that would work together, study together, and evaluate each other's performance. Each syndicate had a chief officer as an assessor, someone whose job it was to observe every part of our conduct and work, on and off duty. As the course was residential during the week, you couldn't fake an attitude, or pretend to be someone you weren't.

One of the assessors was Ranjit Manghnani, a chief superintendent who was temporarily promoted to ACC to be one of the syndicate assessors. I had heard from him before: after the second court case collapsed, he wrote to congratulate me. Perhaps I should have been glad to see him, and even happier when he was made the director of the syndicate I was in. Instead, despite DAC Brown's reassurance, I was thinking: 'If they want to fail me, they are getting an Asian officer to do the job.'

I had emotional baggage, and that's not helpful.

The Senior Command Course is tough – physically, intellectually and emotionally. Four and a half years previously, I had made enemies by criticising the selection process for the course, calling it biased and out of date. Whatever had happened to that process in the time I was away, I couldn't have any complaints about the fairness of the SCC.

It's a crash course in leadership allied to the sort of constant inspection and evaluation that's more reminiscent of a reality TV show than a management training programme. For six months, every week, all week, you are being challenged, graded, questioned and criticised. If one of your colleagues doesn't like your attitude, or thinks you are wrong, they are encouraged to tell you, and tell you why. If you make a presentation, it's their job to question your assumptions. The course is uncomfortable for everyone. Some of the chief superintendents had twenty-five years of service behind them. Some had been in charge of their units for so long that they weren't accustomed to having their decisions questioned. Everyone had a proven track record of high achievement, and they were all far more accustomed to praise than criticism.

It was tough for me for a slightly different reason. When I joined the course, I was thin-skinned, desperate to prove myself right, ready to argue with anyone whose different opinion I thought undermined me. If that had always been my weakness, it was amplified now, and it wouldn't escape the attention of the examiners.

The course breaks all of us down, and rebuilds us from the ground up. It's not enough to have always approached the job in a certain way: we had to be able to explain why we took the decisions we did, and how we made priorities. If we couldn't explain them to each other, we were unlikely to be able to explain them to the thousands of police officers we would be commanding in the future, or to the communities we would be policing. It also attacked head-on the problem that sometimes slows change in the middle ranks of the force: that officers give lip-service to an initiative, pretend to appreciate its importance, while not letting it get in the way of what they consider to be the best way to police operationally. For example, every student on the course has to give a presentation for ten minutes about their strategic vision on their return to their force, what they want to achieve in the next few years. When we studied diversity and inclusiveness on the course, everyone agreed with the aims and the importance of the policy in modern policing. Most of the candidates, however, failed to mention it when asked to present their vision for the future. 'Why not?' the evaluators would ask. 'Don't you think it's important enough to mention?'

Every day, from 9 am to 9 pm, we would gather in our syndicates and work on communications, problem solving, teamwork and strategic thinking, linking it to exercises where we would simulate real command problems. One day we would be listening to a lecture from a government minister; another day we would be discussing the novel *Mary, Queen of Scots*, and what it taught us about the use and abuse of power; and another day we would be simulating how we would cope with an emergency when a hijacked aeroplane needed to be dealt with. We saw more of each other than we saw of our family and friends. I had rarely mixed with police officers after work before, and now there was no one else. And the police officers I was mixing with were my competition, and also the officers who had told me earlier in the day, 'I'm not happy that you talk to me like that. It's insensitive. Don't do it again.' This was feedback that I couldn't brush off.

Although we would be applying for the same jobs after we graduated from the course, we learned to help each other. I have made good friends who had good sense and were honest with me, whether what they told me was good or bad. One day Dave Johnson, a seasoned detective chief superintendent head of CID from Avon and Somerset, told me that he felt like looking under my coat to see if I had another head, because the way I had been portrayed to him before he met me bore little resemblance to what he saw.

I was happy writing essays, doing research, presenting and debating. I had more experience with the law, and could help some of the others when we were living in Fitzwilliam College in Cambridge, using the library every day. Others had twice the length of service that I had, had been detectives or in charge of operational units for so long that they had a deep, instinctive understanding of effective policing. We were all all-rounders, but unless we learned to complement each other and share our knowledge, a tough course would be almost impossible.

It was a hard course, but it was rewarding. One assignment meant visiting another police force to learn about their policing methods and share your thoughts. I visited Dubai, which was off the beaten track, but was an environment in which I felt comfortable, and I also felt that we could learn something about policing other cultures, the sort of information you might not find as easily in Belgium or New York. As the visiting policeman from the UK, I was even interviewed on Dubai television.

Going into the Senior Command Course, most officers are confident, and probably feel there's little they can learn. They are used to giving orders, not taking them, and winning, not being challenged and criticised. It's a mark of the value of the course that we all learn far more about leadership, policing – and ultimately about ourselves. Finally, I learned lessons that had probably held me back since my schooldays.

I learned to network, to make friends that, before, I could tell myself I didn't really need. The course showed me that the world isn't about friends and enemies – and that you should ignore your enemies rather than fight against them. When I was studying to be a barrister, I felt intimidated by my lack of social skills, the sort of skills that others around me seemed to take for granted. For a long time I had convinced myself that I didn't need to make the effort, and perhaps I suffered because I didn't.

I learned a bit of humility too – again, probably a lesson that my colleagues would consider was overdue – and I'm trying to soften my approach to people I disagree with. They might laugh to find out that I've learned to say, 'I may be wrong,' without thinking that it undermines me. Training as a barrister meant

I was good at asking questions, attacking the people I thought were my enemies. Perhaps sometimes I have made enemies where there were none before.

I have also learned the value of compromise: when the neatness of your diary is criticised (as mine was; it's pretty scruffy), then the chief officers who are criticising it as not looking like a chief officer's diary have a point. When my police mentor points out that I cannot just have a career as an NBPA activist, and should try for the highest rank if I really want to change things, I don't think he's trying to muzzle me.

I'm getting the opportunity to put the things I have learned into practice. When the British National Party called ACPO chief Chris Fox a racist, I wrote to the *Guardian* to support him. It's a small gesture, but I hope it's a positive one. Because of my work with the NBPA, very often I have had to disagree with chief constables. I understand now that there are smarter ways to air differences than name-calling. Just because I disagree with some of the ways they go about their business doesn't make them racist. If I was going to make enemies, I'd rather fight a war of words with the BNP.

More importantly, I'm getting the chance to put what I learned into practice on the job. Today, I am a borough commander in the Metropolitan Police, taking charge of policing in a borough called Hounslow. It's an area I'm very familiar with: on the west side, it borders Thames Valley, where I have spent most of my working life as a police officer. On the east, it borders Kensington, where I was working before I was suspended. In the middle, there's Heathrow airport, and areas like Southall and Ealing that I know very well.

Hounslow is huge, exciting, and diverse – just like London. In Hounslow, 144 different languages are spoken. There are 10,000 asylum seekers. It is the leading borough for race hate crime in the UK. One in three of the local councillors are black or

Asian, and in some areas of the borough, two out of three of the population are non-white.

In truth though, Hounslow is simply a microcosm of what every borough in London, and many in the rest of the UK, will look like twenty years from now. It is not a 'problem borough' – it's a huge opportunity to create a police service that works on behalf of the whole community, that recognises which problems are a priority today, and deals with them; that includes, and is accountable to, everyone in the area. If the police force is going to change – as it should – why shouldn't Hounslow lead the way?

For my first 100 days in the job, I changed nothing. I watched, listened, learned. I tried out my new networking skills on the officers I would be working with, and who have admitted since that they were understandably wary of working with me, even positively unhappy about it. I understand better now the benefits of having good friends in the police service regardless of their colour.

Since then, we have put together a programme to measure how well what we do matches what we claim to do. It's called the 'Community Mosaic', because the population of Hounslow is a mosaic, a group of many communities, large and small, rich and poor, with different values and needs. The idea is to show whether our processes, and their results, treat everyone equally, as the law promises they should be treated. It's not just about 'stop and search', and it's not all about race. However we divide up the community, it's right to ask whether we handcuff some groups more than others when we arrest them, and then ask, 'Is there a good reason to do this?' It's OK to ask the questions, 'Do we charge some offenders, and give others a caution, and how do we decide which offenders get which treatment?' We're looking inside the force too – how do we decide who gets promoted, or who is sent on the most prestigious training courses? It's natural for anyone making a decision to favour someone 'like them', but it may not be in the best interests of the force. It's not unusual in the private sector for forward-looking companies to open the promotion process to evaluation. For them, it can mean the difference between commercial success and failure in the next generation. For the police, it can make the difference between a service that reflects the population it is trying to police, or one that is staffed at senior levels by an unrepresentative elite.

At Hounslow we are fortunate to have a professional, effective local police force that is hitting its targets on detection and reduction of crime. In 2005 it was the only borough which achieved its detection targets in London. I am extremely proud of what my colleagues and I have achieved. It gives us the time and authority to ask, 'How can we do this better?' All forces are stretched to the limit to meet these targets, so perhaps if we can uncover ideas that work, we can serve as a template for other forces. Managing our mosaic isn't about being nice to black people. It's ultimately about making the police a legitimate force in our diverse communities, so that those communities can help us to reduce crime and bring offenders to justice.

This isn't about paying lip-service to a political agenda. It's about winning consent from, and the confidence of, our citizens. A police service that does not look like the community it serves – and does not understand the differences among its citizens – will simply not be part of the community. It is a matter of logic. It is communities that defeat criminals and terrorists. After the terrible events of 7 July 2005, the work with our community paid dividends, and was mentioned as an example of good practice in a House of Commons debate into the terrorist threat two weeks later.

Ultimately, it's about having a police service that works as a team, and where the community as a whole can look at a police officer, and say that he or she is 'one of us'.

There's a lot of work to do, but the police force is changing. The Morris Inquiry highlighted the problem that black and Asian recruits are simply not managed, because senior officers are frightened to cause offence. As a result containable problems escalate, fellow officers become resentful at what they see as special treatment, a large number of non-white officers become disillusioned and leave, or simply stagnate in a job that they could be doing better. We can change that, if we recognise that changing it is a priority. As Michael Mansfield pointed out at my trial, if someone had pulled me aside at some point and had been able to talk to me about their concerns about my behaviour, we could have put Helios to bed in a couple of hours, rather than four and a half years, and saved £7 million.

I hope I have learned enough to know that I can't manage the mosaic unless my fellow officers at Hounslow, whatever their background, believe in what we are doing. I have tried to build an environment where they can tell me what they think of my performance. Many already have. I have also tried to build a management structure where I am an officer who happens to be Asian, not an 'Asian officer'. My job is to lead the whole of Hounslow's police force, not just the officers who are the same colour as me.

It will disappoint some of my critics to find out that my lifestyle hasn't changed. I'm divorced from Natalie now, so presumably my children won't have to see my girlfriend described in the press as a 'mistress' any more. I still prefer a nightclub to a pub, and I still socialise with the Iranian community in which I grew up. I still write for the *Guardian* occasionally and sometimes I appear on the TV or the radio to give a view on police matters if I have some knowledge or experience. But spending an extended period of time with my fellow officers taught me that I don't have to live like a monk, worrying in case someone describes my lifestyle as 'unconventional'. I learned enough to know that many police officers, men and women, black, Asian and white, have lifestyles equally as 'unconventional' as mine, as do many millions of adults in the UK today. As long as it doesn't mean I can't do my job, as long as it doesn't affect my judgement or call into question my integrity, it's nobody's business.

Does this sound arrogant? It isn't meant to be. I don't care what the self-appointed knights of integrity led by Chief Supt Norman thought about my unconventional lifestyle. Perhaps they should learn a little about the mosaic and accept that people from London are not necessarily like them. I've been punished for the few things I did and said that I sincerely regret. I have learned a long, hard lesson, and I just hope that other people don't have to learn by having their private lives, their phone calls, their eating habits and their relationships paraded in national newspapers and on television.

And what has happened to the officers behind Helios? The time since my court case has not been as kind to them. The Essex police force has been asked to carry out an inquiry into the conduct of Helios, one whose remit stretches from beginning to end of the story. It is even investigating the conduct of two Metropolitan Police commanders who were asked to investigate Helios after the second court case collapsed, asking whether they did their duty at the time. In a strange reversal of fortune, Chief Supt Norman, who so delighted in handing me my disciplinary notices over breakfast in the Meridien Hotel in Slough, has now been forced to fight his way through a blizzard of Reg 9s questioning his conduct during Helios, his treatment of witnesses, and his lines of inquiry.

In December 2006, the Investigatory Powers Tribunal – headed by a high court judge – found that the bugging of my phone during Operation Helios was unlawful. Helios officers had eavesdropped as black and Asian police officers discussed potential action against their bosses for racial discrimination when I was acting as a legal advisor to the NBPA – but, in the words of the tribunal, they had 'no lawful grounds' to do so. The NBPA had always claimed this was a breach of legal professional privilege, violating their right to privacy, and now we have been vindicated.

I still get hate mail, one or two a month. Before I took the job at Hounslow, a senior officer warned me that there was still a small hard core of objectors who would 'like to see me die', but they are not currently much in evidence. Recently another senior officer came to see how I was doing in Hounslow. We went for a walk and coffee in the shopping centre. What was the secret behind the success of the work we are doing in the borough, he asked me? I invited him to look around and tell me how many people in the shopping centre looked like him, and how many looked like me. I suggested that the residents of the borough could often recognise their experience in mine, and sometimes that made it easier for me to explain and deliver the Met's priorities in a way they understood.

He saw the predominately Asian and black people in the shopping centre. 'I get the point,' he said.

Diversity is not a beauty contest; it works. When someone writes to tell me to 'fuck off back to my own country', I wish I could show him the borough in which I work. He would see how we work together to police the whole of the population, and how we support each other, regardless of our background or colour. Then I can say to him, and people like him, that there's nowhere for me to go back to. In today's London and today's Metropolitan Police, I'm one of us.